I0491089

ART BOOKS

FROM CRESCENT MOON PUBLISHING

BURNE-JONES

BURNE-JONES

By A. Lys Baldry

CRESCENT MOON

First published 1909. This edition © 2020.

Set in Book Antiqua 10 on 14pt.
Designed by Radiance Graphics.

Thanks to the authors and publishers quoted.

British Library Cataloguing in Publication data

ISBN-13 9781861716460

CRESCENT MOON PUBLISHING
P.O. Box 1312, Maidstone, Kent, ME14 5XU
Great Britain, www.crmoon.com

CONTENTS

NOTE ON THE TEXT

The text is from *Burne-Jones* by A. Lys Baldry, published by Frederick A. Stokes, New York, 1909.

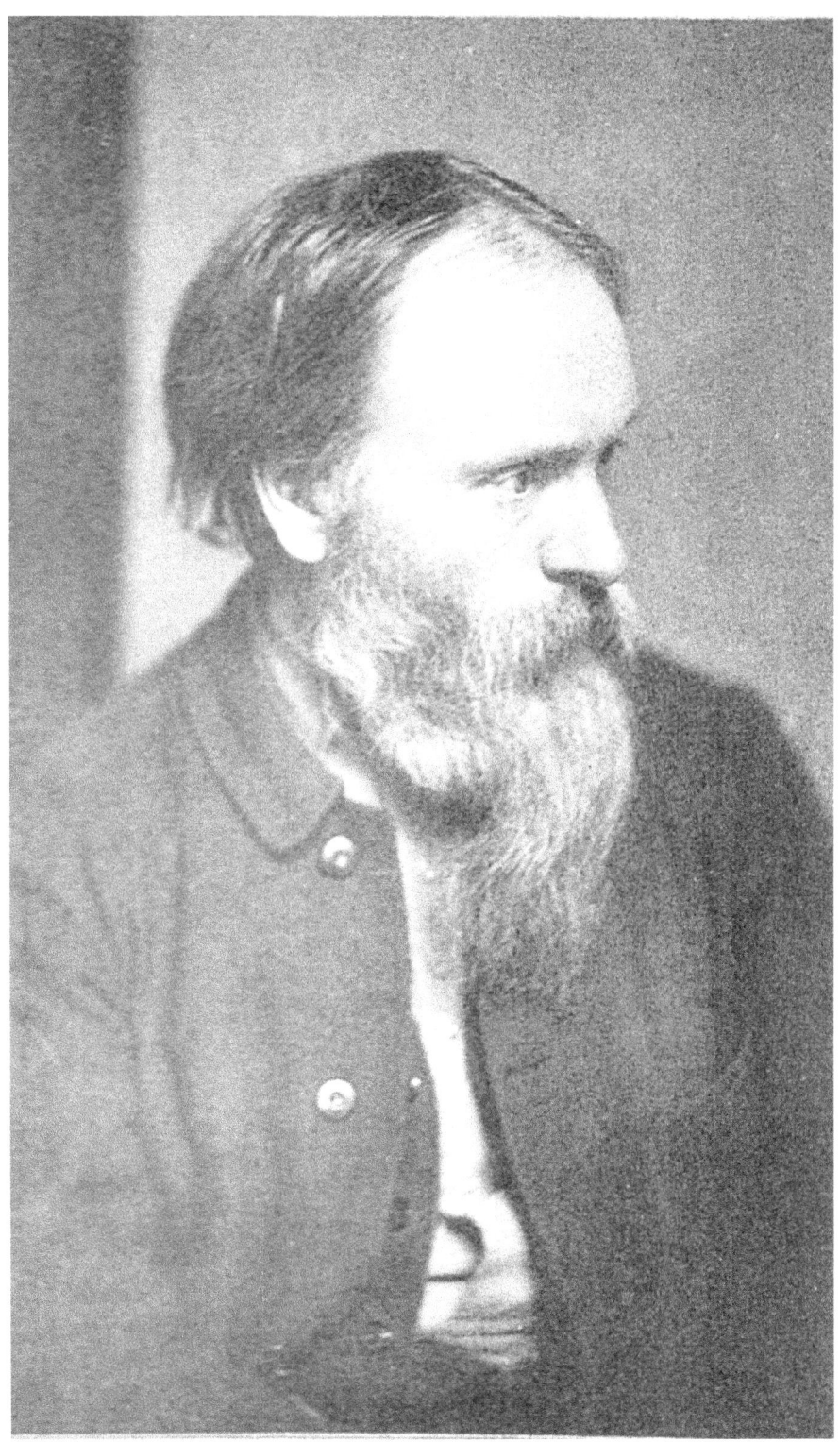

Edward Burne-Jones, portrait by Frederick Hollyer, c. 1882

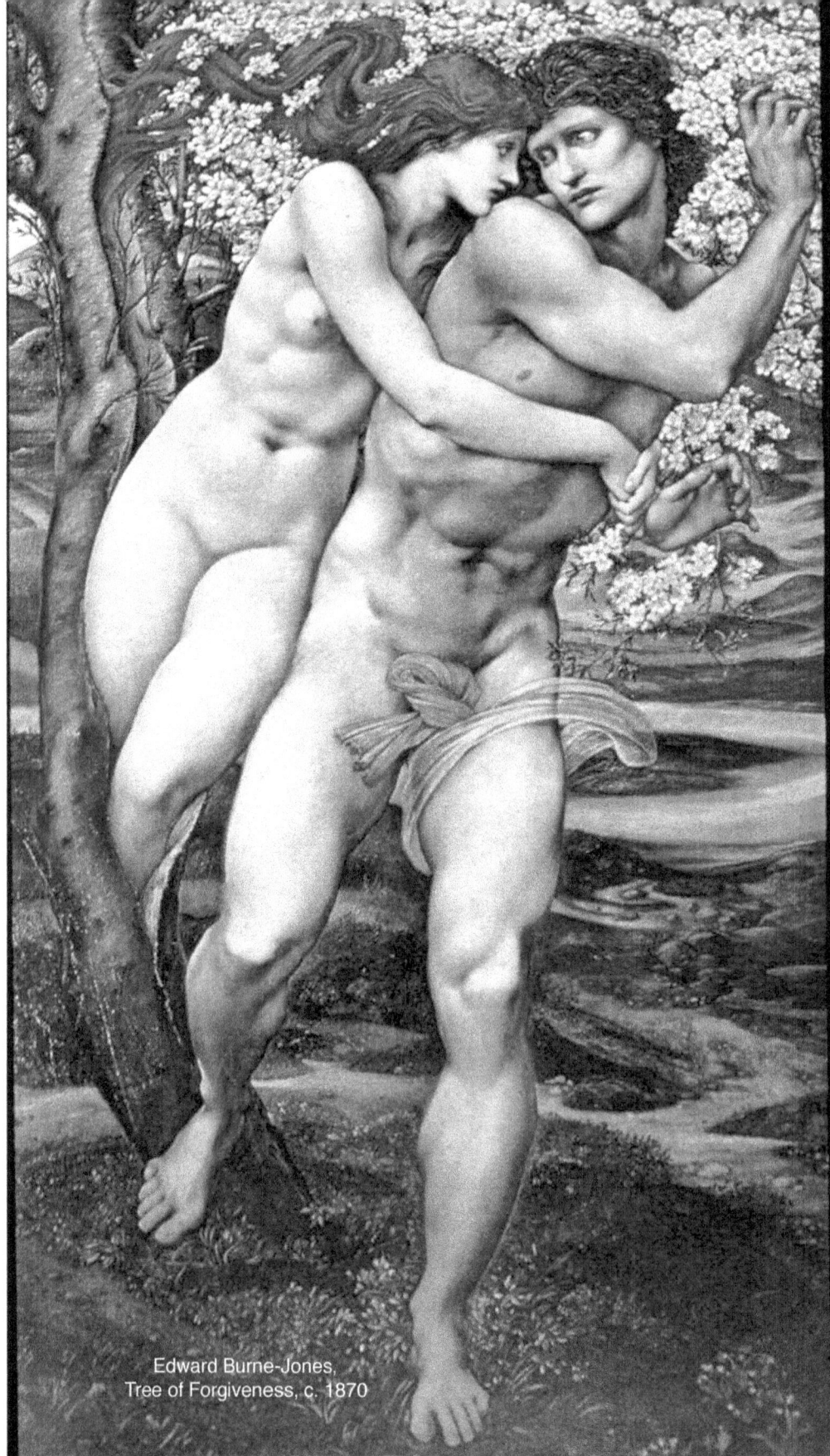

Edward Burne-Jones,
Tree of Forgiveness, c. 1870

The place which should be assigned to Sir Edward Burne-Jones in the history of modern art is by no means easy to define, for his work with its unusual qualities of intention and achievement does not lend itself readily to classification. At the outset of his career he might with some justice have been numbered with the Pre-Raphaelites, because the first influences to which he responded were those which directed the Pre-Raphaelite movement, and because in his earliest productions he showed that these influences had counted for much in the shaping of his æsthetic inclinations. But as he developed he made plainer and more convincing the assertion of his individuality, he ceased to be simply a follower of a movement, and evolved for himself a system of æsthetic practice which was personal both in aim and in manner of expression. That in formulating this system he borrowed much from early Italian art, that he based himself upon certain remote masters, with whose primitive methods he was deeply in sympathy, can scarcely be denied; but in this reference to the past he did not show the blind readiness to imitate which is the vice of the copyist; he altered and adapted, varied this principle and modified that detail, until he had with the material he collected built up a quite complete superstructure, which was Italian only in its foundation. And in this process of building up he was guided surely enough by a right instinct for decorative propriety, an instinct which was partly innate, partly the outcome of associations by which he was largely affected throughout his life. If his personality had been less strong, or his æsthetic preference less defined, these associations might easily have cramped his imagination and narrowed him into the repetition of a set formula; but his intelligence was so keen and his conviction concerning his artistic mission was so clear, that he was able to overcome all the obstacles by which he might have been turned from his right course. His career, thanks to the consistency with which he worked, became a record of continuous effort to realise an ideal that lacked neither nobility nor intellectual variety.

It is probable that some of his consistency, and a very large part of his artistic conviction, came from the manner of his preparation for the profession in which he attained such exceptional success. Unlike most artists he did not begin by acquiring a knowledge of the mechanism of painting, and did not proceed to apply trained technical skill in experiments intended to determine the direction in which he might practise profitably in after life. In his case the process was reversed, for his direction was settled before he had learned even the rudiments of pictorial practice, and the time which other men would have given to experiment he devoted to seeking how he would best realise the ideas that were finally formed in his mind. Tentative work, to test the popular point of view, he never produced; he began straight away with what he knew to be his right material, and the only difference which is to be noticed between his first and his last paintings is a difference in technical facility. The uncertainties of handling in his earlier pictures disappeared in those which he painted in later life, but of mental uncertainty no trace is at any time to be discovered.

Yet the curious fact must be noted that this artist, with his strong personality, his great gifts, and his absorbing devotion to a splendid ideal, chose his profession by a kind of afterthought – almost by accident. There is no record in his case of a boyhood spent in struggles against a fate which seemed to forbid him all satisfaction of his dearest aspirations; there is not even evidence that he had any artistic aspirations at all. He grew up, practically to manhood, before he discovered that he had either the wish or the capacity to attempt any form of æsthetic expression, and his powers lay completely dormant through all those youthful years which have been to most other artists a time of longing after the apparently unattainable and of striving to follow the promptings of nature and temperament.

This strange torpidity of the artistic side of his intelligence was, no doubt, due to the surroundings among which he passed his childhood. He was born on August 28, 1833, at Birmingham, where there was in those days little enough to foster a love of art, and in the respectable but dull atmosphere of a middle-class home he had no chance of any awakening. His mental activity, however, was shown in the zest with which he threw himself into the study of the classics during the seven or eight years that he spent at King Edward's School. He gained at that time a very thorough knowledge of the classic writings in general and of classic mythology in particular, which was amplified in after life by constant reading; and he acquired a student-like habit of research into the learning of the past which served him well when the time came for him to picture the fancies that were forming in his mind.

But at first the purpose of his education was to fit him for the walk of life which his father wished him to follow. He was, it was decided, to enter the Church, and in 1853, having won a scholarship at Exeter College, he went up to Oxford ready and willing enough to work for success in the profession which seemed so well suited to him. He had at that time no feeling that his real vocation lay in quite another direction, or that there was any different way in which his studious mind might be exercised. The idea of taking orders was not uncongenial to him, and he began his Oxford life in no spirit of rebellion against the career which had been mapped out by his elders.

At Oxford, however, came his awakening. He found himself in contact there with quite a new phase of existence, in an atmosphere which was made doubly impressive by its unlikeness to any that he had previously known, and among surroundings which by their novelty had a great power to stimulate his imagination. Under such conditions the expansion of his mind was unusually rapid, and the arousing of his dormant æsthetic instincts followed immediately. This latter development of a side of his nature, of which previously he could have been, at best, only dimly conscious, was greatly assisted by his friendship with a remarkable man who had entered Exeter College on the same day that he did, and who had come to Oxford with the same intention of eventually taking holy orders. This man, William Morris, was destined to play a most important part in British art activities, and by his militant æstheticism to bring about many momentous changes in the public taste; and the chance which brought him and Edward Burne-Jones together, when they were both at the most impressionable period of life, was especially fortunate.

The association between the two undergraduates quickly became one of the closest intimacy. They had mentally much in common, and in them both was a strain of enthusiasm and poetic fantasy which was an inheritance from a Celtic ancestry – they were both Welshmen by descent – and by which their whole attitude to modern existence was determined. Morris had, perhaps, the more vehement personality and the greater share of the fighting instinct, while Burne-Jones was more of a dreamer and readier to occupy himself with abstract fancies; but these small differences of temperament made their friendship the more mutually valuable, and helped appreciably to increase the influence which the one had on the other. At any rate, these days at Oxford saw the beginning of a kind of mental partnership which gave ultimately to the world a great artist and a brilliant leader of a wide art movement which has since done much to alter the whole spirit of domestic decoration in this country.

A more immediate effect of the intimacy between Morris and Burne-Jones was, however, the weakening of the intention which had brought them to the university. The more they dreamed and talked the further their idea of finding a career in the Church receded, and the stronger grew the desire which both of them felt for the pursuit of some form of art. While they were thus hesitating over their plans for the future, Burne-Jones received a sort of revelation which fixed finally his half-formed intention to become a painter. He saw by chance some works by Rossetti, an illustration to a poem by William Allingham and a water-colour, "Dante's celebration of Beatrice's Birthday," and these, with some notable Pre-Raphaelite pictures, like Holman Hunt's "Light of the World" and "The Christian Priest escaping from the Druids," which were then at Oxford, gave him a veritable inspiration. For Rossetti in particular he conceived immediately a passionate adoration, and to sit at the feet of such a master seemed to him the noblest aim in life. From that moment, indeed, his fate was decided, though some little time had yet to elapse before his dreams could be realised and his plans could be put into working shape.

For the abandonment of all the ideas which had brought him to the university was no small matter and not to be lightly undertaken. He had to think of the disappointment at home which such action on his part would cause, and he had also to consider what would be his own position while he was preparing himself for a profession of which he had not so far had the smallest practical experience. So, with little heart in his work, he went on reading for his degree until the winter of 1855, when he came up to London with the intention of seeing in the flesh the man whom he had hitherto worshipped afar off. He was introduced to Rossetti at the house of Mr. Vernon Lushington, and by the kindly painter, who discerned the promise in the young man's tentative drawings, he was given the heartiest encouragement. A little later he laid before Rossetti all his hopes and fears, his doubts whether or not he would be right in leaving Oxford with the purpose which had taken him there still unfulfilled, and his desire to devote himself irrevocably to the artistic calling; and instead of suggestions of such compromises as prudence might have dictated, he received advice to lose no time in entering upon the career for which he was plainly destined by nature and inclination.

Rossetti's interest in his young admirer was no momentary matter; he backed up the advice he had offered by taking him as a pupil and by aiding him in many ways to gain a footing in the art world. When Burne-Jones, having at last shaken the dust of Oxford off his feet, settled in London early in 1856, he found Rossetti quite ready to supervise his education and to lead him to that fuller knowledge of art practice which he so sorely lacked. The method of education adopted departed very definitely from accustomed lines; it did not involve attendance at any art school, and it imposed no prolonged course of drawing from antique figures or of painting still-life studies from groups of ill-assorted objects. On the contrary, the pupil was encouraged to begin at what would be considered by academic teachers the wrong end of things – to struggle, all unversed as he was in technicalities, with the difficulties of creative effort. Rossetti's studio was thrown open to him so that he might watch the progress of the pictures which were on the easel, and a number of the master's drawings and studies were lent to him to help him in his work at home; but what training he received was more in the nature of sympathetic guidance in his attempts at self-expression than of formal direction along the lines of a recognised school system. Its good effects were shown in the manner of the young man's development and in the rapid growth of his individuality; its bad effects in the persistence of defects of draughtsmanship and brushwork, which were overcome at last by his extraordinary industry and dogged determination to master all the difficulties of his craft.

To his care and advice concerning his pupil's manner of working Rossetti added consideration for his financial position. Burne-Jones, with but slender resources and with little chance as yet of earning the means of support, was having a somewhat hard struggle, which Rossetti did his best to relieve by introducing him to friends who would interest themselves in him, and by helping him to get such work as he was capable of carrying out. One important commission was obtained about the end of 1856, and this commission deserves special mention because it gave Burne-Jones his first experience in a branch of design in which he was destined to become an acknowledged master. Messrs. Powell, the glass-makers, who were making great efforts to improve the quality of stained glass, had applied to Rossetti for a design for a window. He declined to undertake this work, and recommended his pupil instead; and Burne-Jones accordingly prepared a design which was not only accepted by the firm but enthusiastically approved by Ruskin, who was, so Rossetti declared in a letter written at the time, "driven wild with joy" by the merit and quality of the work. This cartoon was followed during the next three or four years by several others drawn for the same firm.

Much that is important in the record of the painter's life is to be assigned to this short period between the beginning of 1857 and the end of 1860. In addition to his designs for stained glass, he produced a large number of pen-and-ink and water-colour drawings, and made his first experiments in oil-painting; and he took part in the decoration of the library of the Oxford Union, an ambitious scheme entered into by Rossetti at the suggestion of Mr. Woodward, the architect of the building, and carried out, despite many unexpected difficulties, by Rossetti himself and a band of enthusiastic young artists. These decorations, which unfortunately fell into a condition of hopeless decay soon after they were completed, took some six months to execute, and he was engaged upon his share of the work until the early part of 1859. In the autumn of that year he paid his first visit to Italy and studied those early Italian masters with whom, as his after work proved, he was so deeply and intelligently in sympathy. This visit, indeed, brought about a marked change in his artistic outlook and helped to lead him away from the Gothic tendencies which he had first shown – probably as a result of his association with Morris – into a far more pronounced inclination for the Italian manner of design. He was married in the summer of 1860 to Miss Georgina Macdonald, about a month after Rossetti's marriage to Miss Siddal; and in taking this step he certainly showed that he had confidence in his professional prospects, a confidence which was justified by the position he had already made for himself.

The year 1861 must be particularly noted because it marks the commencement of an undertaking with which Burne-Jones was closely associated for the rest of his life. William Morris, who had also left Oxford in 1856 without waiting to take his degree, had gone for rather less than a year into the office of George Edmund Street, the well-known architect, with some idea of adopting that profession; and then, becoming quickly disillusioned, had after some experiments in painting settled down for a while to literary work. In 1859 he married and went to live in a house which had been built for him at Bexley Heath; and it is said that the difficulty he experienced in getting, for the fitting up of this house, things which would please his fastidious taste and gratify his intense love of beauty, induced him to consider whether he could not actively intervene in the much-needed reformation of the decorative arts. At any rate, less than two years after his marriage, he was busy with the details of a scheme which was ambitious enough to satisfy even his love of big things and in which there were endless possibilities.

This scheme took definite form towards the end of 1861, when the firm of Morris, Marshall, Faulkner, and Co. was started in Red Lion Square. Burne-Jones, naturally enough, was an active sympathiser with the plans of William Morris, and he showed his sympathy in the most practical manner by putting his talents as a designer at the disposal of the firm. From that time onwards he produced in ever-increasing numbers designs for all kinds of decorative work, stained glass, tapestries, embroideries, book illustration, &c., in which his amazing fertility of imagination and exquisite powers of expression had the fullest scope. The sum total of the work, for which he was responsible during the period of nearly forty years over which his intimate connection with the Morris business extended, was almost incredibly large, and proves convincingly the strenuousness of his lifelong effort.

For it must be remembered that this mass of decorative work did not by any means represent the whole of his achievement, but was, in fact, brought into existence in the intervals of his not less remarkable activity as a picture painter. The number of his finished pictures in different mediums was about two hundred, and his cartoons for stained glass alone make a list of a thousand or more; when to these are added his designs for other purposes, his sketches and studies, and the rough notes by which he gave the first visible shape to the mental images which he proposed to put later on into a completed form, the result arrived at is simply bewildering. Only by the most unremitting industry could he have done so much, and only a man with an abnormally prolific imagination and extraordinary powers of invention could have kept up as he did the high standard of his art.

The pictorial work of Burne-Jones during the earlier 'sixties marked well the manner in which he was finding his way to the full avowal of his artistic creed. At first he was, as might have been expected, frankly inclined to imitate Rossetti, and to follow closely in methods and sentiment the master whom he worshipped and from whom he had received such invaluable assistance. But gradually this influence waned, as increasing confidence in his own powers enabled him to assert more clearly his individual view of his æsthetic responsibilities, and as the widening of his experience opened up to him fresh aspects of the artistic problems with which he had to deal. His development was, no doubt, much assisted by a second visit which he paid to Italy in the spring of 1862, a visit in which he had as his companion Ruskin, with whom he was by then on terms of intimacy. He stayed first at Milan and then went on to Venice, where he remained for some while making copies of Tintoretto and other masters for Ruskin, and studying for his own instruction and enjoyment the works of the earlier masters generally and of Carpaccio particularly.

During these earlier years he confined himself almost entirely to working in water-colours, though by his way of using the medium he gained technical results which had more the strength and richness of oils than the delicate transparency of water-colour. The few essays he made in oil-painting at this time were not pictures for exhibition purposes but pure decorations, like the panels for a painted coffer designed by William Morris, and a triptych, with the "Annunciation" as the central panel, and the "Adoration of the Magi" on the wings, which was commissioned by Mr. Bodley for St. Paul's Church at Brighton. Definite recognition of the position he had gained among the younger water-colourists came at the beginning of 1864, when he was elected, with Fred Walker, an associate of the Royal Society of Painters in Water Colours. He was advanced to full membership of the Society in 1868, but resigned in 1870 because a foolish accusation of impropriety was brought against one of the compositions he exhibited. He returned, however, in 1886 and remained a member till his death.

By the paintings he showed in the gallery of the "Old Society" he much increased his reputation among discriminating art lovers as an artist of no ordinary importance. People who had known nothing of his work before found something so new in manner and so distinctive in purpose in the achievements of this creator of poetic fantasies that he was given more attention than usually comes to a man who sets before the public things of an unaccustomed type. That he amply deserved this attention cannot be questioned, for already he had acquired sufficient command over the technicalities of water-colour to enable him to put into a quite convincing form fancies which needed particular delicacy of interpretation. Of course, he had still very much to learn – no one knew better than he did how necessary was strenuous labour to overcome his deficiencies as a craftsman – but his deep sincerity gave character and meaning to his paintings, and the poetic beauty of his pictorial inventions fully excused what defects there were in his executive methods.

Indeed, to this early period can be assigned several of the works on which his reputation rests most securely to-day – his "Fair Rosamond," for instance, his first painting of "The Annunciation," a subject which he treated more than once, and his exquisite picture of "The Merciful Knight," in which there was no trace left of Rossetti's direction, but instead a clear expression of a quite personal view of art. No better proof could have been given of the strength of his character than was afforded by the rapidity with which he found his own way, and by the completeness of his emancipation from the influence of a man who was both his master and his friend – an influence which plainly dominated him when he painted his earliest water-colours of "Clara von Bork" and "Sidonia von Bork," both of which were entirely in Rossetti's manner. But in the three or four years which intervened between the production of these two little pictures and the completion of the far more ambitious composition, "The Merciful Knight," he had learned the secret of his own powers, and he had found how unnecessary it was for him to lean for support upon any one else.

With this knowledge of himself, and with this consciousness of his capacity to take an independent position in the art world, came an increase of his activity as a painter. His water-colours became more numerous and more important, and he began to paint in oils several large pictures which he worked at with characteristic patience, setting them aside often for quite considerable periods and returning to them every now and again as opportunity offered. His manner of working, indeed, showed plainly the fertility of his mind; new ideas occurred to him in rapid succession, and his habit was to put them into a first rough shape on paper or canvas and to leave them to be carried to completion by slow stages with often long intervals between. One result of his method was that he frequently repeated the same subject with variations in treatment that were the outcome of some fresh consideration of the motive – each repetition, however, was an independent conception, not a mere reproduction of what he had done before.

But there was another result which must be noted, because it has to be taken into account in any attempt to make a chronological list of his paintings or to define the character of his art at different periods – the works he exhibited were not put before the public in anything like the order of their production.

Sometimes a picture which had been painted only a few months before was shown with one which had been for years in his studio awaiting some comparatively small additions to bring it to absolute completeness; sometimes all the things he exhibited in a particular year were new works; sometimes old ones which had been taken up and put aside over and over again. Consequently, it is useless to try to classify his productions exactly, and it is hopeless to base any theories about his development as an artist upon the sequence of his public appearances. All that can be said is that his evolution was steady and progressive, and that his apparent reversions now and again to his earlier manner were due not to any halting in his conviction but simply to the fact that some piece of work which had been lying by, possibly for years, had at last been finished and exhibited. Practically the only periods which can be recognised in his art are the comparatively brief one when he was definitely under Rossetti's influence, and the far longer one when he was working out his own destiny unassisted. A certain inclination towards Rossetti's colour feeling he retained for some while after he had freed himself of the technical mannerisms which he derived from his master, and for nearly twenty years traces of this colour sympathy can be detected, but for the rest of his career he was as individual in his management of colour as he was in design or in the sentiment of his work.

This point needs to be elaborated for the sake of clearing up any misapprehensions which might arise from his more or less erratic way of exhibiting his work. As an example, when he exhibited for the first time in 1864 in the gallery of the Royal Society of Painters in Water Colours, he showed the "Fair Rosamond," painted in 1862, with the "Annunciation" and "The Merciful Knight," both of which belong to 1863; but in 1865 he sent "A Knight and a Lady," finished just before the exhibition opened, "Green Summer," painted in 1863, and "The Enchantments of Nimue," which was one of the things he produced in 1861 while he was still frankly and unreservedly an imitator of Rossetti. Such an inversion in the order in which his works were set before the public might cause some perplexity to students of his art if they did not realise what was his custom in this matter.

He exhibited in the gallery of the Royal Water Colour Society in 1869 a painting, "The Wine of Circe," which was not only the most important work he had produced up to that time but is also to be counted as one of the most admirable of all his performances; and he showed there in 1870 two other notable works, "Love Disguised as Reason" and "Phyllis and Demophoon." It was over this last painting that the dispute arose which led to his resignation of his membership of the Society; and one of the results of this dispute was that for a space of seven years hardly any of his pictures were seen in public. Indeed, the only things he exhibited during this period were a couple of water-colours, "The Garden of the Hesperides" and "Love among the Ruins," which appeared at the Dudley Gallery in 1873. Both were important additions to the list of his achievements, and the "Love among the Ruins" especially was a painting of exquisite beauty and significance. He repeated this subject in oil some twenty years later, because the original water-colour had been damaged somewhat seriously, and was not, as he considered, capable of repair.

The opening of the Grosvenor Gallery in 1877 gave him his first great opportunity of setting before the mass of art lovers his claims to special attention. Hitherto he had counted in the minds of a few men of taste and sound judgment as an artist of remarkable gifts who promised before long to take high rank in his profession, but by the larger public interested in art matters he was practically undiscovered. That he would have won his way step by step to the position he deserved cannot be doubted; if there had been no break in his activity as an exhibiting painter his successive contributions to the Royal Water Colour Gallery could not have failed to make him widely known. But his reappearance at the Grosvenor Gallery was so dramatic, and so convincing in its proof of the amazing development of his powers, that he leaped at one bound into the place among the greatest of his artistic contemporaries, which he was able to hold for the rest of his life without the possibility of dispute.

For he had not been idle during this seven years of abstention from exhibitions; the period had been rather one of strenuous activity and unceasing production. It saw the completion of several important canvases on which he had laboured long and earnestly, and it saw the commencement of many others which were in later years to be added to the list of his more memorable achievements. In some ways, indeed, it was a fortunate break; it saved him from the need to strive year by year to get pictures finished for specific exhibitions, and it allowed him time for calm reflection about the schemes he desired to work out. It freed him, too, from the temptation – one to which all artists are exposed – to modify the character of his art so that his pictures might be sufficiently effective in the incongruous atmosphere of the ordinary public gallery. He was able to form his style and develop his individuality in the manner he thought best; and then at last to come before the public fully matured and with his æsthetic purpose absolutely defined.

When the first fruits of this long spell of assiduous effort were seen at the Grosvenor Gallery, Burne-Jones became instantly a power in the art world. The judgment of the few connoisseurs who had hailed "The Wine of Circe" and "Love among the Ruins" as works of the utmost significance, and as revelations of real genius, received wide endorsement; and though some people who were out of sympathy with the spirit of his art were quite ready to attack what they did not understand, their voices were scarcely heard amid the general chorus of approval. Indeed, for such pictures as "The Days of Creation," "The Mirror of Venus," and "The Beguiling of Merlin," exhibited in 1877; "Laus Veneris," "Chant d'Amour," and "Pan and Psyche," which with some others were shown in 1878; the series of four subjects from the story of "Pygmalion and the Image," and the magnificent

"Annunciation," in 1879; and that exquisite composition, "The Golden Stairs," which was his sole contribution to the Grosvenor Gallery in 1880, nothing but enthusiastic approval was to be expected from all sincere art lovers; to carp at work so noble in conception and so personal in manner implied an entire want of artistic discretion.

There were two exhibitions at the Grosvenor Gallery in 1881. In the summer one Burne-Jones was not represented, but the winter show included a number of his studies and decorative drawings, among them the large circular panel, "Dies Domini," a water-colour of rare beauty which can be reckoned as one of the most admirable of his designs. In 1882, however, he showed "The Mill," "The Tree of Forgiveness," "The Feast of Peleus," and several smaller paintings; and in 1883 that splendid piece of symbolism, "The Wheel of Fortune," and "The Hours." The following year is memorable for the appearance of the important canvas, "King Cophetua and the Beggar Maid," and the less ambitious but even more fascinating "Wood Nymph," in both of which the artist touched quite his highest level of achievement, and gave the most ample proof of the maturity of his powers.

His election as an Associate of the Royal Academy came in 1885. That he coveted this particular distinction can scarcely be said; indeed, he was at first unwilling to accept it, and it was only in response to a personal request from Leighton that he finally decided to take his place in the ranks of the Associates. But he exhibited a picture at Burlington House in 1886, "The Depths of the Sea," and then, feeling that his work was unsuited for the Academy galleries, he sent nothing else there, and in 1893 resigned his Associateship. His contributions to the Grosvenor Gallery in 1886 were "The Morning of the Resurrection," "Sibylla Delphica," and "Flamma Vestalis"; and in 1887 "The Baleful Head," "The Garden of Pan," and some other canvases.

After this year he ceased to exhibit at the Grosvenor Gallery, as he was one of the chief members of the group of artists who supported Mr. Comyns Carr and Mr. C. E. Hallé in the founding of the New Gallery, and he sent there nearly all the works he produced during the rest of his life. The most important exceptions were the magnificent "Briar Rose" series of pictures, which were shown in 1890 by Messrs. Agnew at their gallery in Bond Street, and "The Bath of Venus," which went straight from the artist's studio to the Glasgow Institute in 1888.

The first exhibition at the New Gallery was opened in 1888, and it included several of his oil-paintings, among them "The Tower of Brass," an enlarged repetition of an earlier picture, and two canvases, "The Rock of Doom" and "The Doom Fulfilled," from the "Story of Perseus" series, to which also belonged "The Baleful Head," shown in the previous year. To the succeeding shows there he sent much besides that can be taken as representing his soundest convictions. There were the large water-colour, "The Star of Bethlehem," and the "Sponsa di Libano," in 1891; "The Pilgrim at the Gate of Idleness" and "The Heart of the Rose" in 1893; "Vespertina Quies" and the oil version of "Love among the Ruins" in 1894; "The Wedding of Psyche" in 1895; "Aurora" and "The Dream of Launcelot at the Chapel of the San Graal" in 1896; "The Pilgrim of Love" in 1897; and "The Prioress' Tale" and "St. George" in 1898. In all of these his consistent pursuit of definite ideals, his love of poetic fantasy, and his admirable perception of the decorative possibilities of the subjects he selected are as evident as in any of his earlier works; as years went on he relaxed neither his steadfastness of purpose nor his sincerity of method. To the last he remained unspoiled by success and unaffected by the popularity which came to him in such ample measure – it may be safely said that with his temperament and his artistic creed he would have continued on the course he had marked out for himself even if the effect of his persistence had been to rouse the bitterest opposition of the public, and he was as little inclined to trade on his success as he would have been to tout for attention if his efforts had been ignored.

There was no waning of his powers as his career drew towards its close. It was not his fate to be compelled by failing vitality to be content with achievements that lacked the force and freshness by which the work of his vigorous maturity was distinguished, for he died before advancing years had begun in any way to dull his faculties. Only a few weeks after the opening of the 1898 exhibition at the New Gallery he was seized with a sudden illness, which had a fatal termination on the morning of June 17. Really robust health he had never enjoyed, and on several occasions serious breakdowns had hampered his activity; but his devotion to his art was so sincere, and his determination so strong, that these interruptions did not perceptibly affect the continuity of his work. Towards the end of his life, however, he suffered from an affection of the heart, and the demands which he made upon his strength helped, no doubt, to exhaust his vitality. At the time of his death he was striving to complete one of the most important and ambitious pictures he ever planned – "Arthur in Avalon," a vast canvas which, even in its unfinished condition, must be reckoned as an amazing performance, and worthy of a distinguished place in the record of modern art.

One of the most interesting things in the life-story of Edward Burne-Jones is the manner of his advance, within some twenty years only, from a position of obscurity to one of exceptional authority in the British school. The young student, who in 1855 had just discovered his vocation and was beginning to feel his way under the guidance of Rossetti, had become in 1877 one of the most discussed of British artists, and had with dramatic suddenness entered into the company of the greatest of the nineteenth-century painters. With no effort on his part to attract attention, without having recourse to any of those devices by which in the ordinary way popularity is won, he secured, practically at the first time of asking, all that other men have had to strive for laboriously through a long period of probation. Although the few things he exhibited while he was a member of the Royal Water Colour Society were sufficient to rouse in the few real judges a deep interest in his future achievement, it was the singular merit of his contributions to the first exhibition at

Grosvenor Gallery that made him instantly famous. The wider public realised then, and realised most forcibly, that he was an artist to be reckoned with, and that his work, whether people liked it or not, could by no means be ignored.

From that time onwards there was for him no looking back. The twenty years of preparation, which were spent mainly in ceaseless seeking after completer knowledge and in careful study of the practical details of his profession, were followed by another twenty years of strenuous production, in which he worked out more and more effectively the ideas formed in his extraordinarily active mind. In the series of his paintings there is a very perceptible advance year by year in technical facility, but to suggest that they show also a growth of imaginative power would scarcely be correct, because there seems to have been no moment in his career when he did not possess in fullest measure the faculty of poetic invention and the capacity to put his mental images into an exquisite and persuasive shape. What he acquired as a result of his exhaustive study was a closer agreement between mind and hand, the skill to convey to others what he himself felt. But he had no need to labour to make his intelligence more keen or his fancies more varied; nature had endowed him with a temperament perfectly adapted for every demand which he could make upon it in the pursuit of his art.

That he did not at first secure the unanimous approval of art lovers is scarcely surprising. The markedly individual artist who cares nothing for popular favour and is more anxious to satisfy his own conscience than to gather round him possible clients is never likely to become a favourite offhand. Burne-Jones by the brilliancy of his ability silenced all opposition long before his death, and gained over the bulk of the doubters who questioned his right to the admiration he received when he first began to exhibit at the Grosvenor Gallery. But for some while the unusual character of his art caused it to be much misunderstood by people who had not taken the trouble to analyse his intentions. He was accused of affectation, of deliberate imitation of the early Italians;

he was attacked for his indifference to realism and for his decorative preferences. Even the genuineness of his poetic feeling was suspected, and his love of symbolism was ridiculed as the aberration of a warped mind. Much of this misconception was cleared away by the collected exhibition of his works which was held at the New Gallery in the winter of 1892-1893, for this show, by bringing together the best of his productions and by summing up all phases of his practice, proved emphatically that he had been as sincere and logical in his aims as he had been consistent in his expression. It was no longer possible to attack him out of mere prejudice; the verdict given fifteen years before on his art by those who understood him best was seen to be just. When a second collection was shown at the New Gallery – a memorial exhibition arranged in 1898, a few months after his death – few people remained who were prepared to dispute his mastery.

It is fortunate that justice should have been done to him by his contemporaries and that there should have been really so little delay in the wider acknowledgment of his claims. If appreciation had been withheld from him while he lived, if it had been his fate to secure only a posthumous reputation, there would have been some diminution of his influence, and his art would have lost some of its authority. But as a right estimate of his position was arrived at during his lifetime, when he was at the height of his activity as an exponent of an exceptionally intelligent æsthetic creed, he was able to make his beliefs effective in bringing about the conversion of a large section of the public to a truer understanding of the value of decorative qualities in pictorial art. He proved emphatically that decoration does not imply, as is popularly supposed, the abandonment of the characteristics which make a picture interesting; he showed that a subject can be legitimately treated so that it engages fully the sympathies of the average man, and yet can be kept from any descent into obviousness or commonplace conventionality. The painted story in his hands was no trivial anecdote; it was a motive by means of which he conveyed not only moral lessons but artistic truths as well, something didactically valuable but at the same time capable of appealing to the senses with exquisite daintiness and charm.

Indeed, he can best be summed up as a teacher who clothed the lessons of life with noble beauty and with dignity that was commanding without being forbidding. There was human sympathy in everything he painted – a tender, gentle sentiment which escaped entirely the taint of sentimentality and which, tinged as it always was with a kind of quiet sadness, never became morbid or unwholesome. He was too truly a poet to dwell upon the ugly side of existence, just as he was too sincerely a decorator to insist unnecessarily upon common realities. That he searched deeply into facts is made clear by the mass of preparatory work he produced to guide him in his paintings, by the enormous array of drawings and studies which he executed to satisfy the demand he made upon himself for exactness and accuracy in the building up of his designs. But in his studies, as in his pictures, the intention to express a personal feeling is never absent. He selected, modified, re-arranged as his temperament suggested; he omitted unimportant things and amplified those which were of dominant interest; he sought for what was helpful to his artistic purpose and passed by what would have seemed in wrong relation, consistently keeping in view the lesson which he desired to teach. It can be frankly admitted that a certain mannerism resulted from his way of working, but this mannerism was by no means the dull formality into which many artists descend when they substitute a convention for inspiration; it was rather a revelation of his personality and of that belief in the rightness of his own judgment which counts for so much in the development of the really strong man. Except for the short time in which he was influenced by Rossetti, his life was spent in illustrating an entirely independent view of artistic responsi-bilities; and it would be difficult now to question this independ-ence with the wonderful series of his paintings available to prove how earnestly and how seriously he strove to realise his ideals in art.

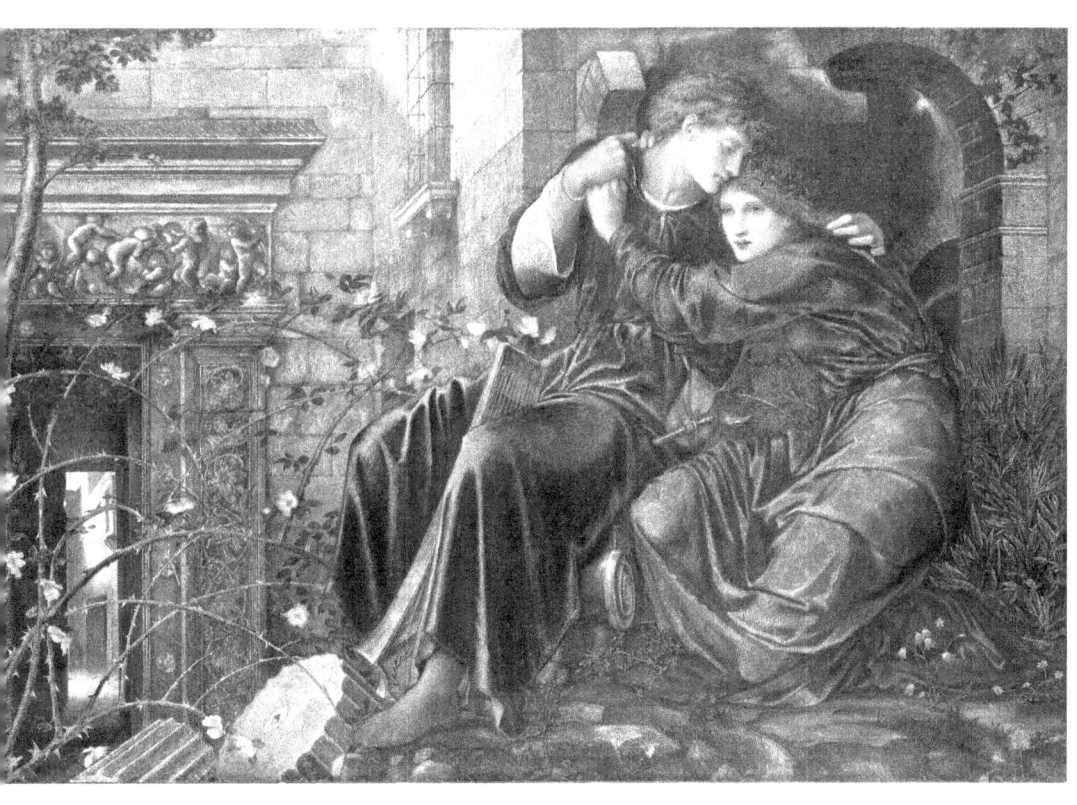

Edward Burne-Jones, Love Among the Ruins, 1873

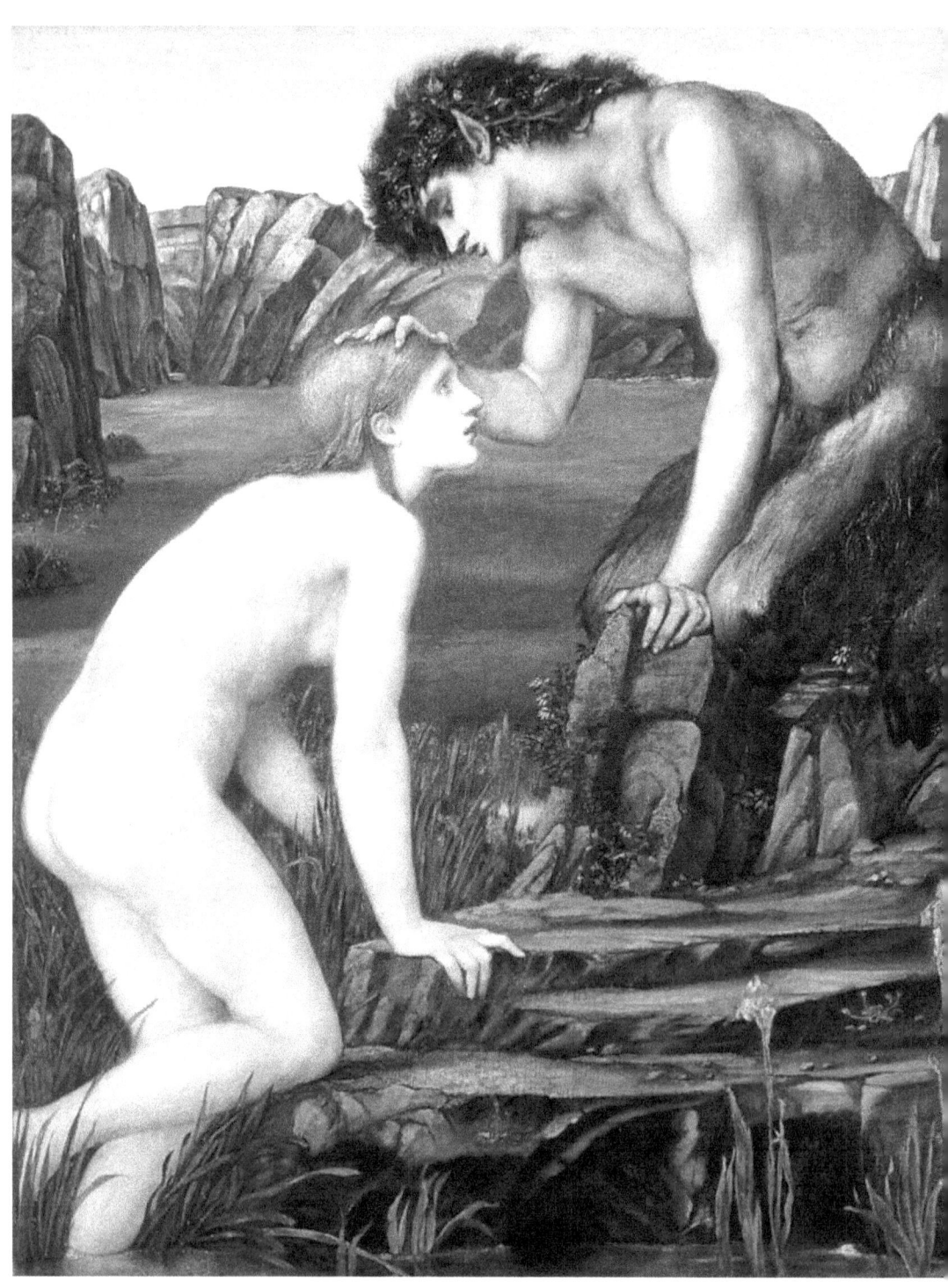

Edward Burne-Jones, Pan and Psyche

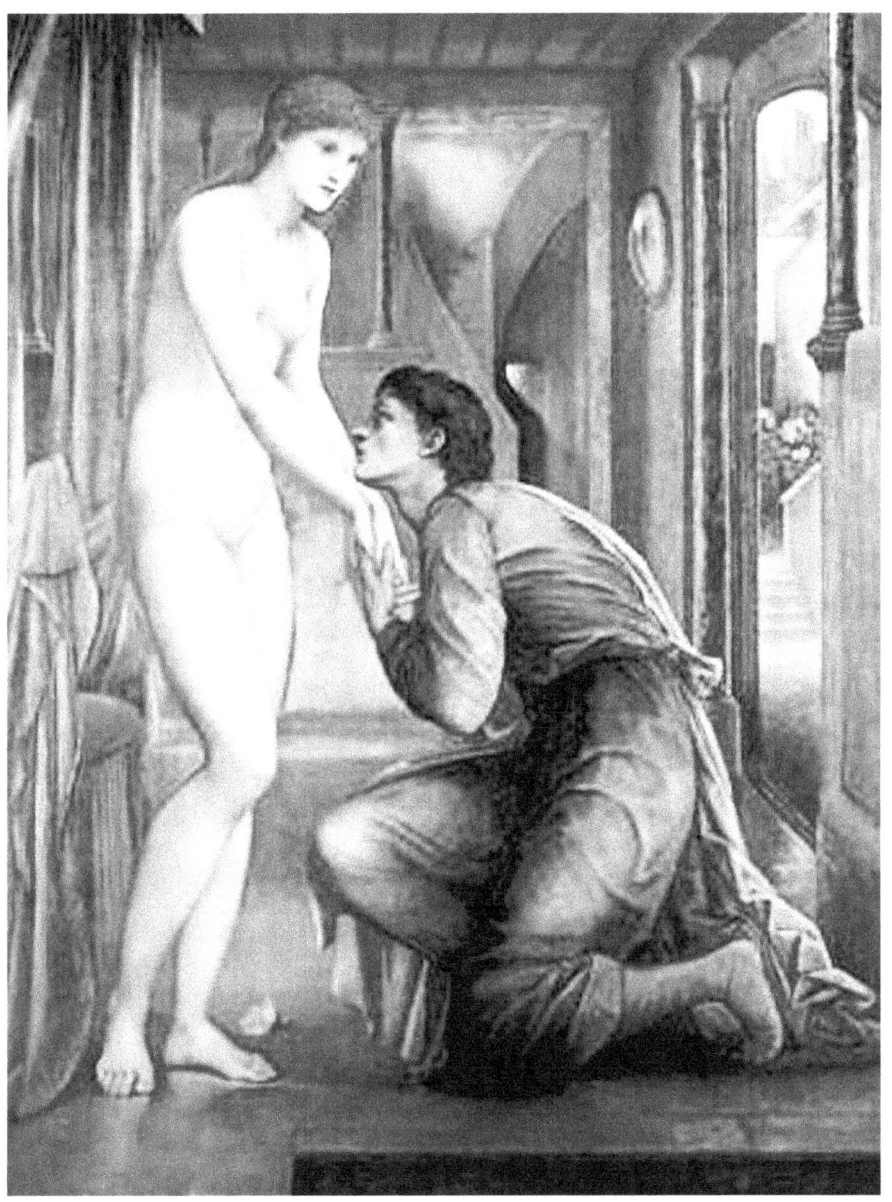

Edward Burne-Jones, Pygmalion, 1878, Birmingham, England

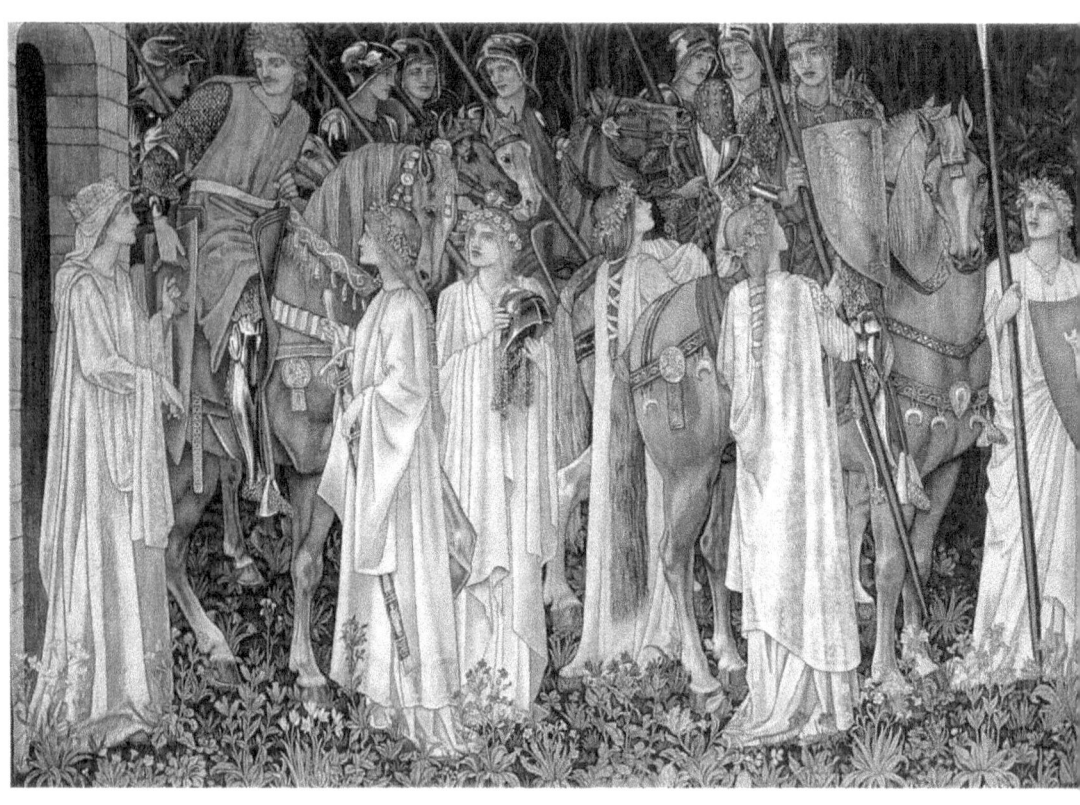

Edward Burne-Jones, Holy Grail Tapestry,
The Arming and Departure of the Knights, 1890s

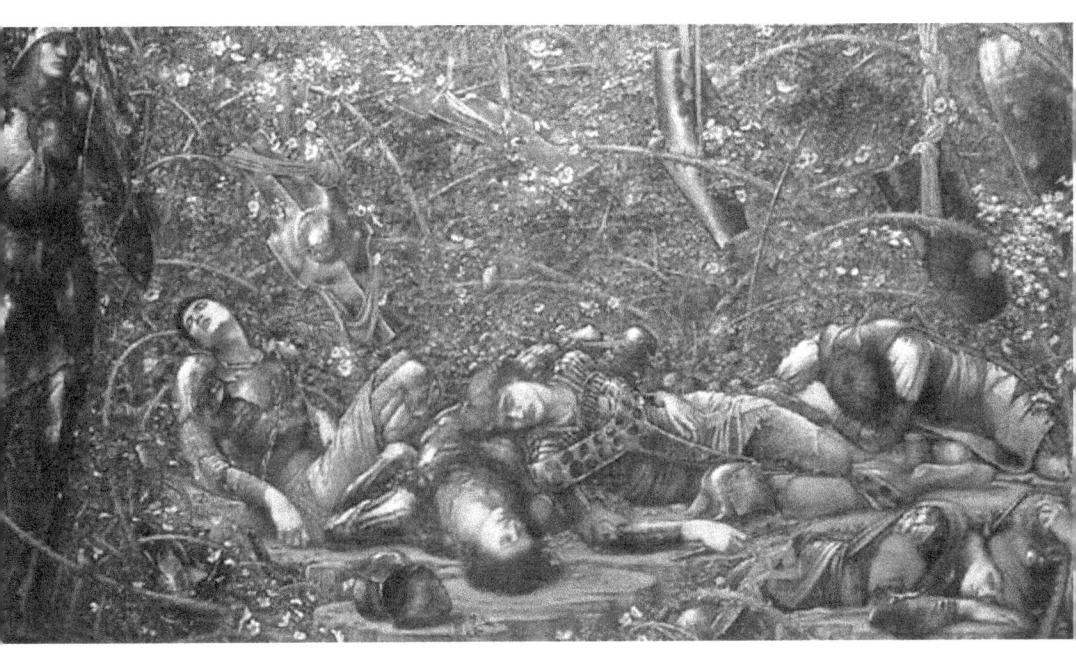

Edward Burne-Jones, Briar Wood, Buscot Park

Edward Burne-Jones, Last Sleep of Arthur In Avalon

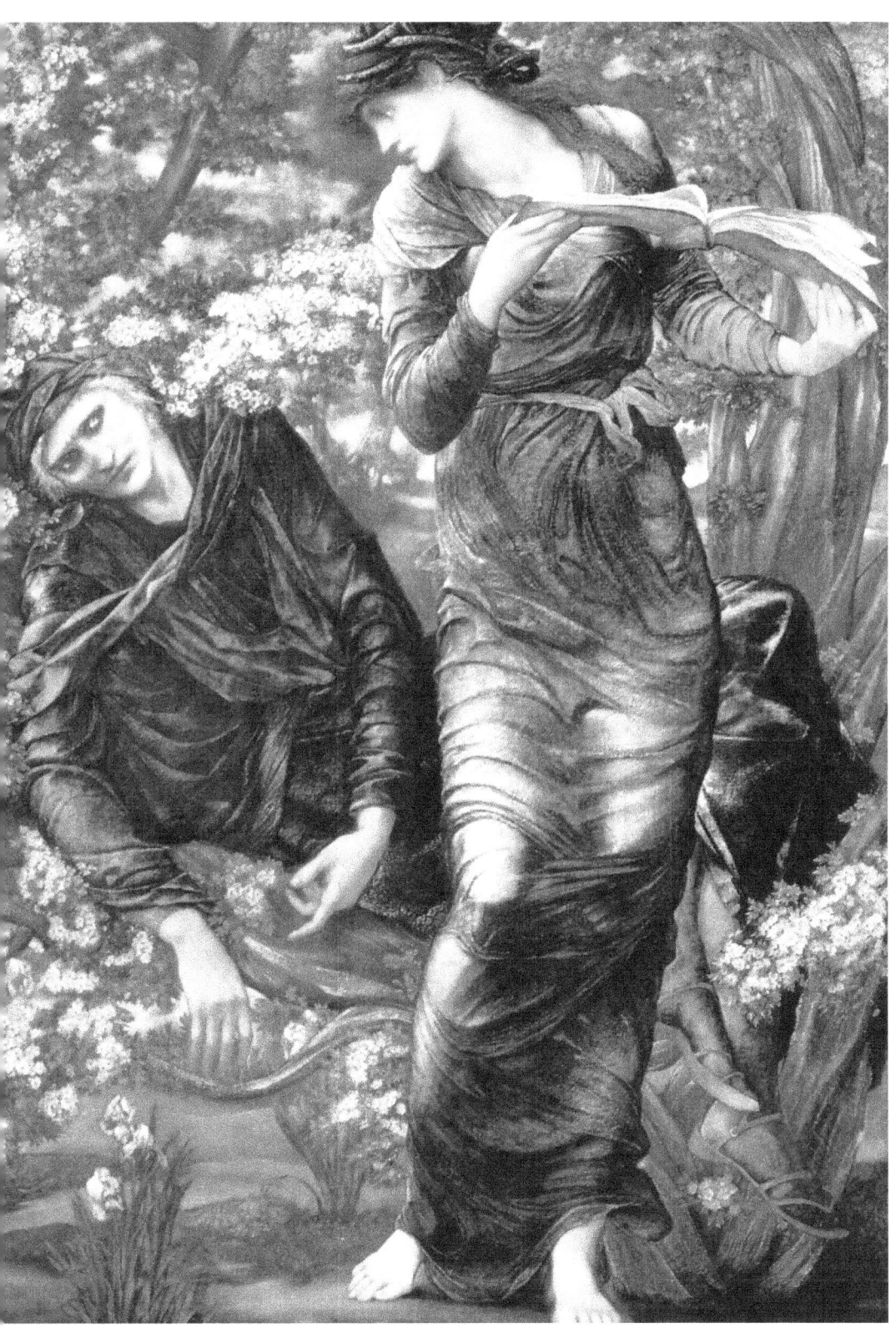

Edward Burne-Jones, The Beguiling of Merlin

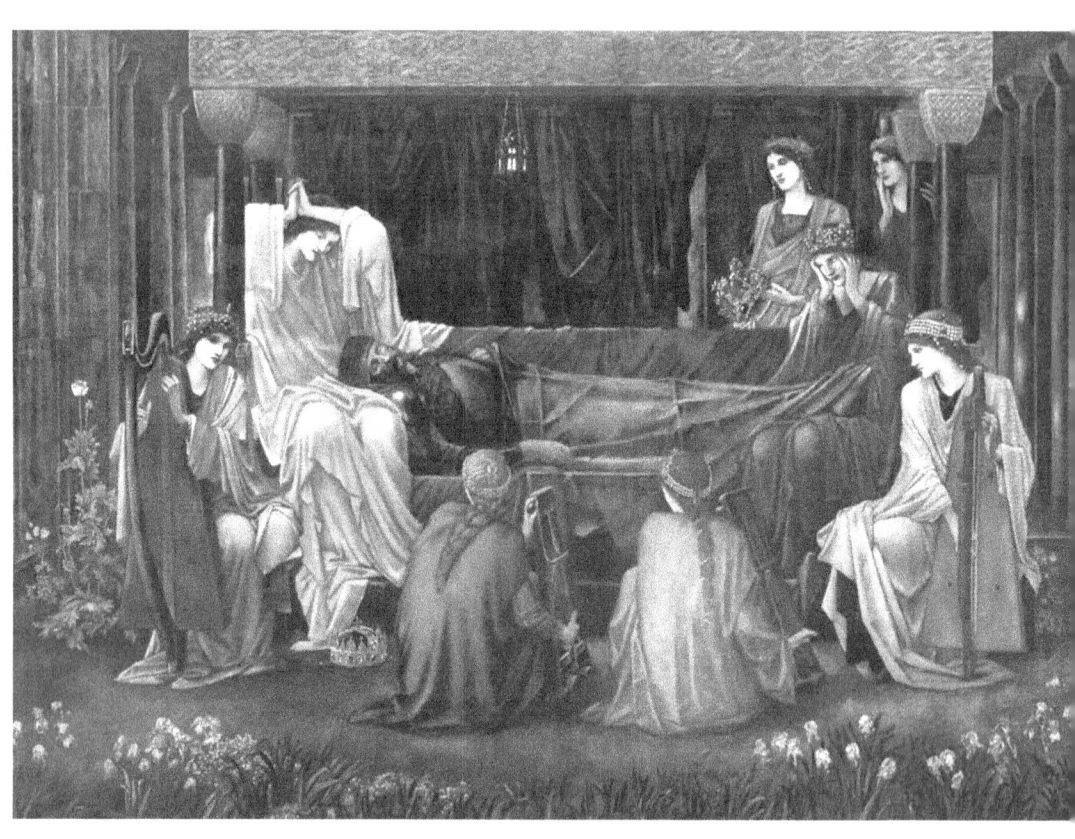

Edward Burne-Jones, The Last Sleep of Arthur, 1898

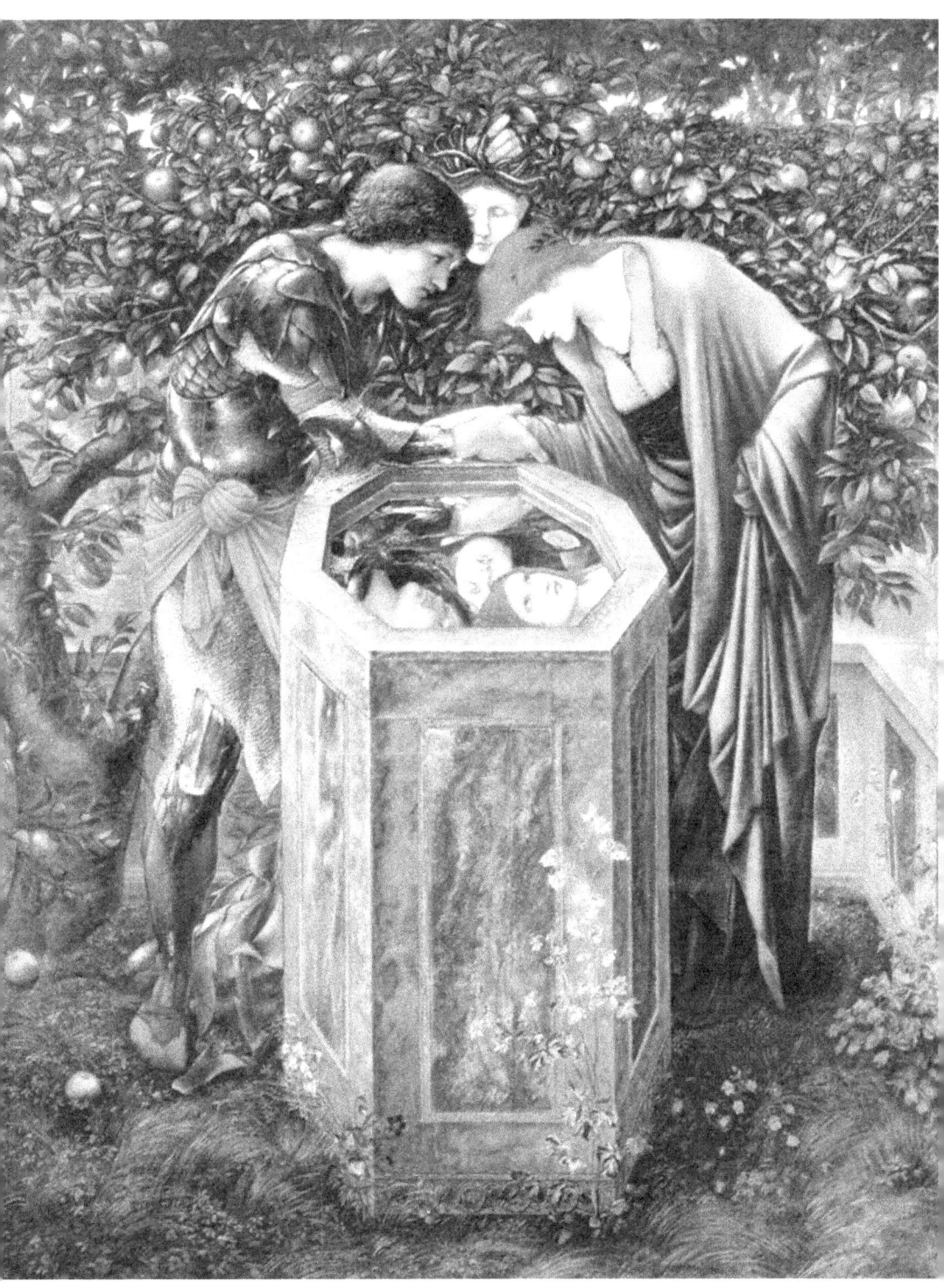

Edward Burne-Jones, The Baleful Head, 1887

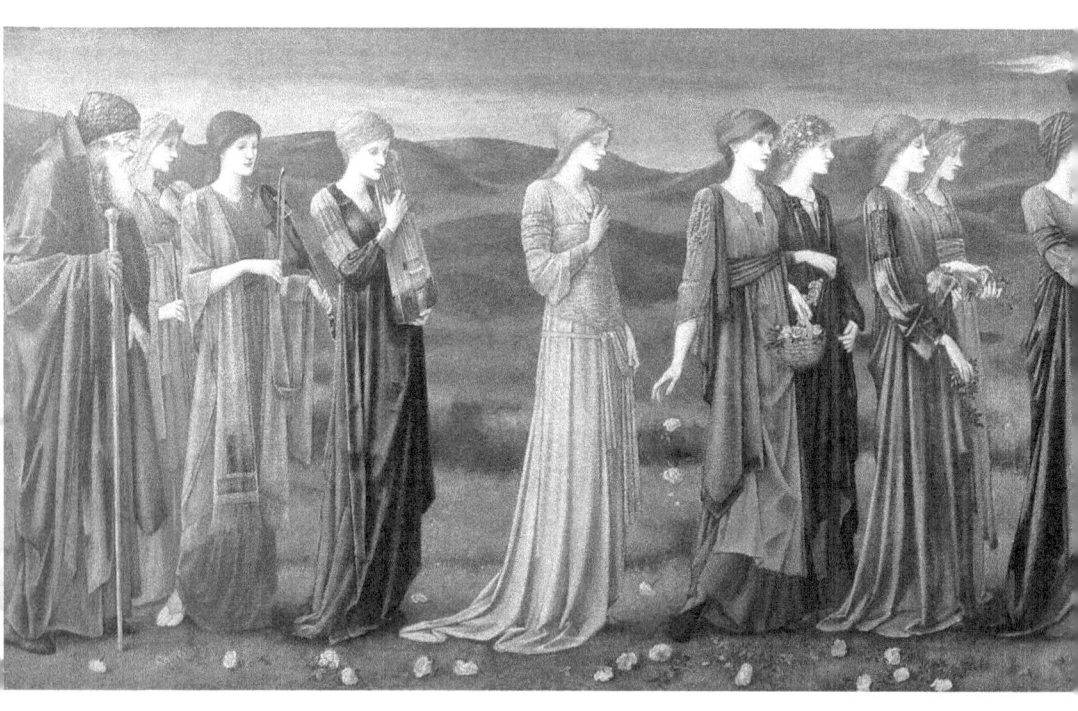

Edward Burne-Jones, Psyche's Wedding, 1895

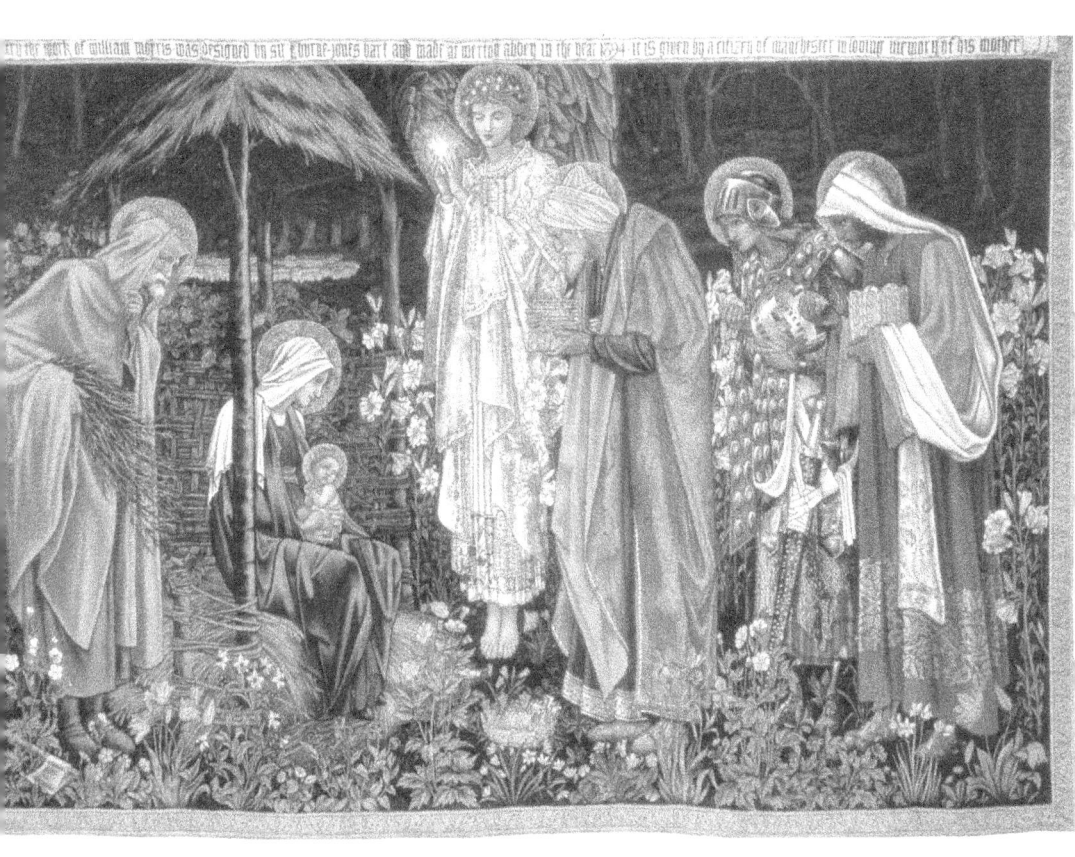

Edward Burne-Jones, Adoration of the Magi, tapestry, 1894

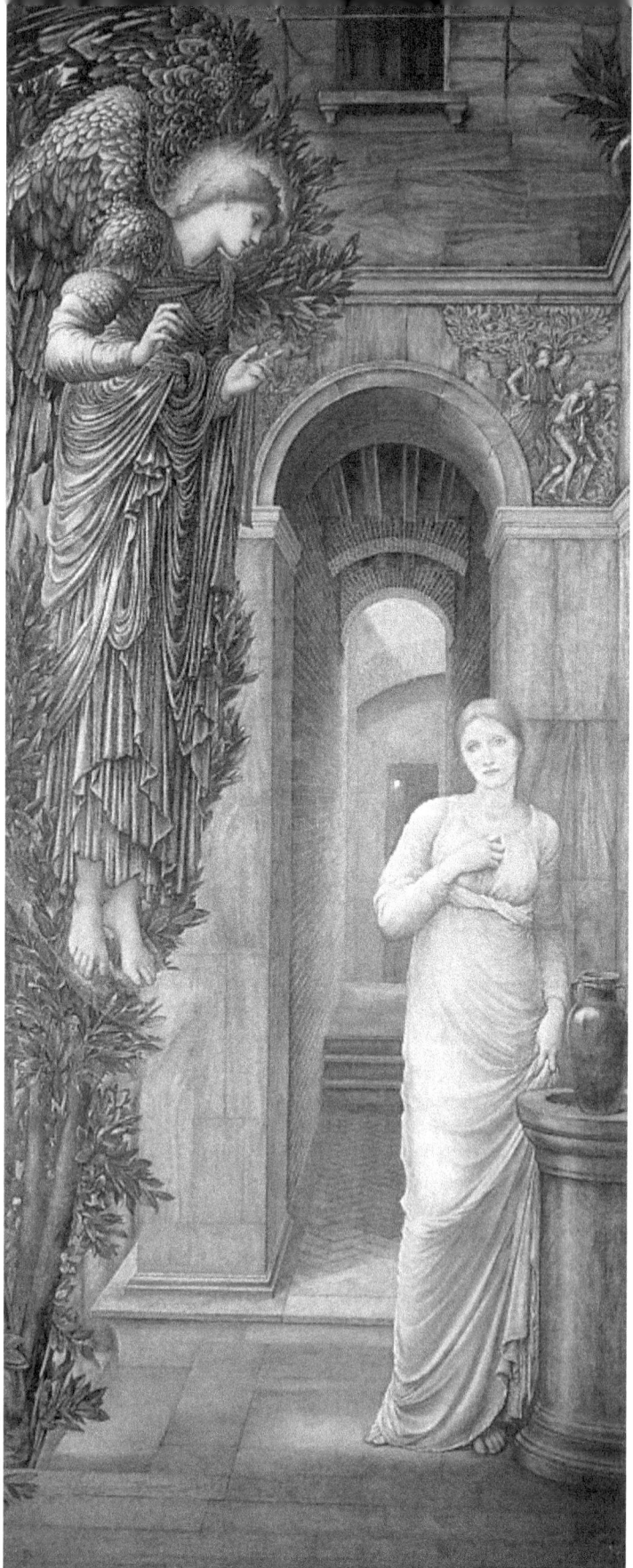

Edward Burne-Jones,
Annunciation, 1879

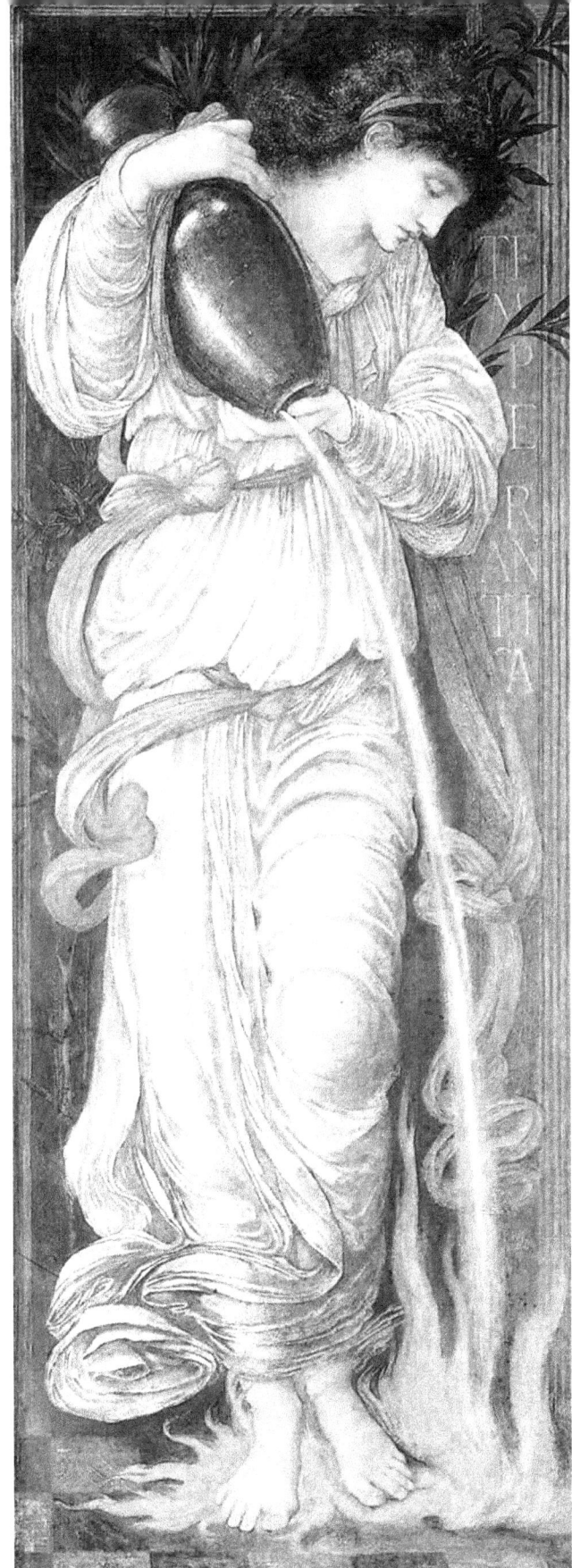

Edward Burne-Jones,
Temperantia, 1872

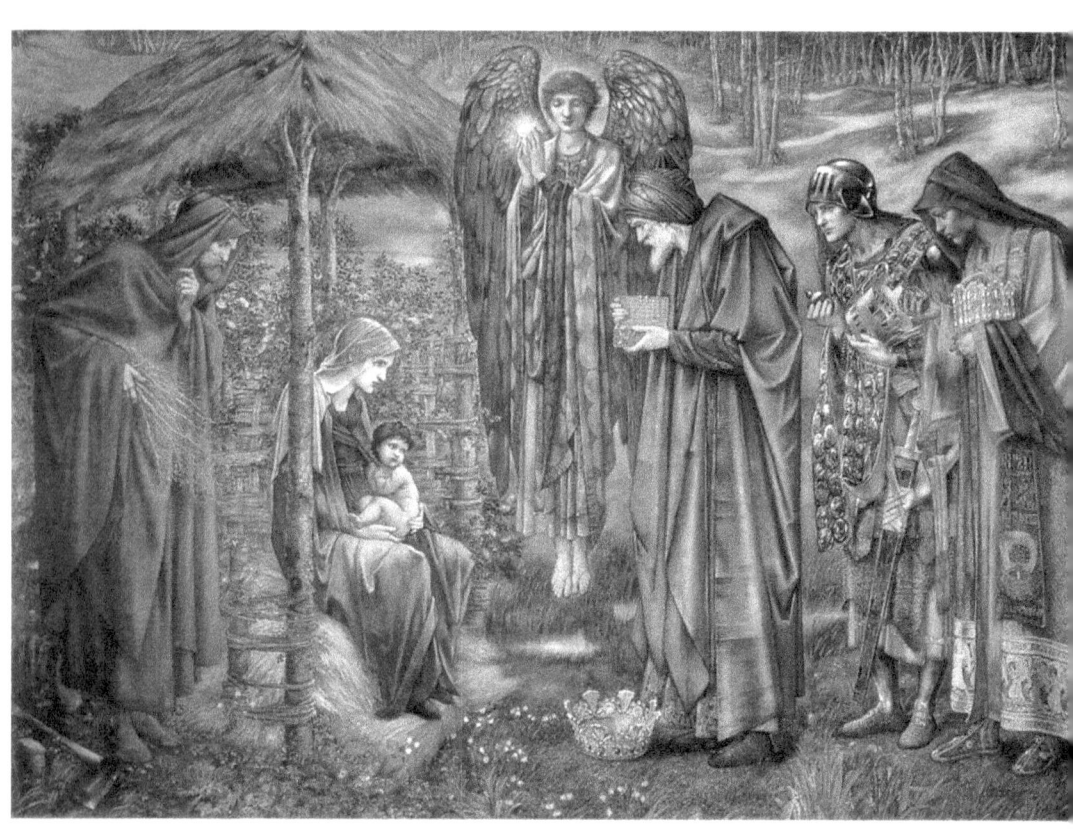

Edward Burne-Jones, Star of Bethlehem, 1890

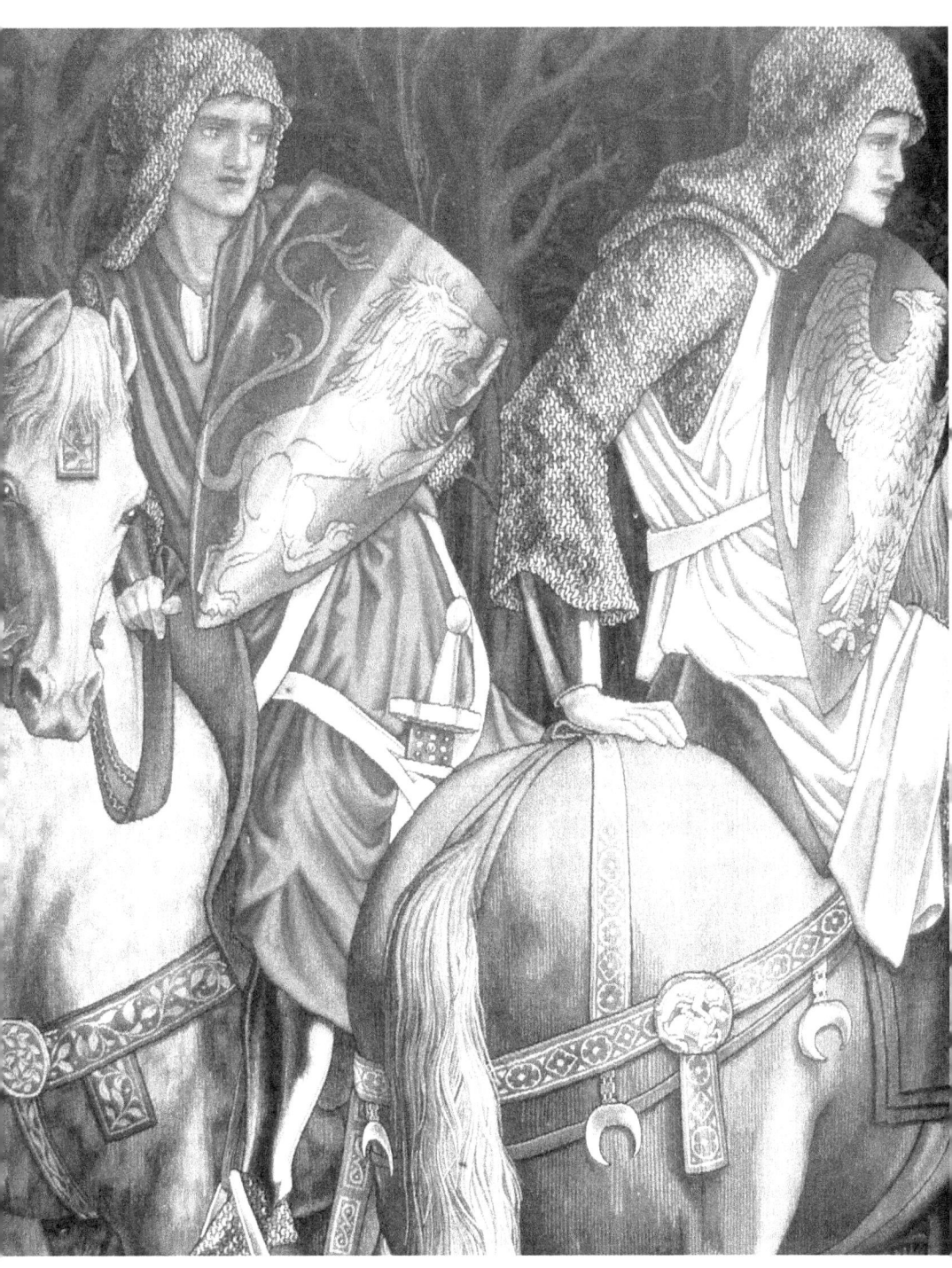

Edward Burne-Jones, Quest For the Holy Grail Tapestries, 1895

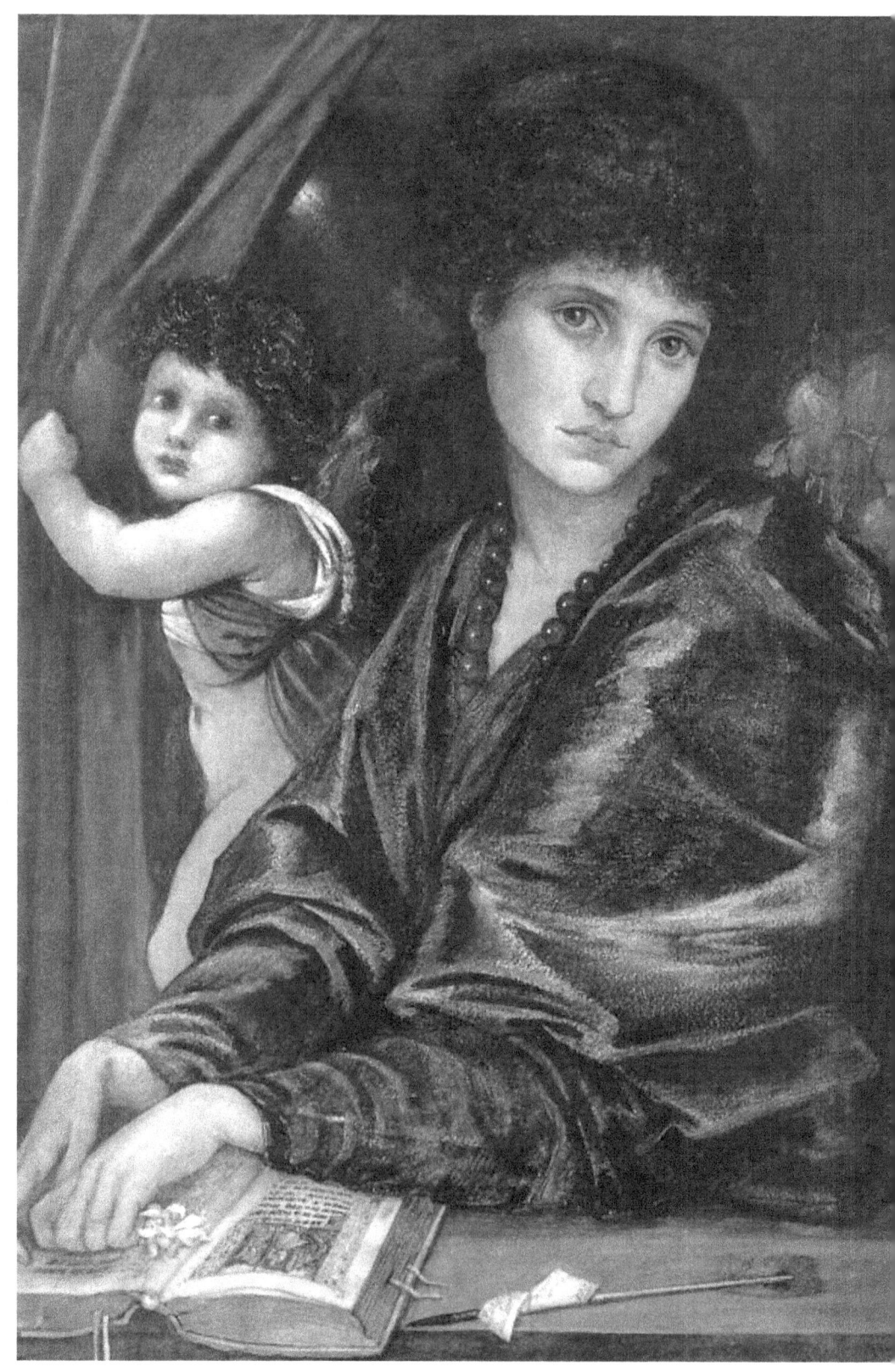

Edward Burne-Jones, Maria Zambaco, 1870

NOTES ON WORKS

THE DEPTHS OF THE SEA.
(In the possession of R. H. Benson, Esq.)

Apart from its technical beauty and its charm of design, this picture has a special interest as the only contribution which the artist ever made to the exhibitions of the Royal Academy. It was shown at Burlington House in 1886, and was painted purposely, during the months that intervened between his election as an Associate in the summer of 1885 and the opening of the 1886 exhibition. In the treatment of the subject there is a touch of slightly grim humour, unusual in the art of Burne-Jones, a humour which finds expression particularly in the face of the mermaid, who drags a human being to her cave at the bottom of the sea without thinking or caring that her sport means death to him.

SIDONIA VON BORK
(In the possession of W. Graham Robertson, Esq.)

As an early picture, painted while Burne-Jones was still under the influence of Rossetti, "Sidonia von Bork" illustrates characteristically a particular phase of the artist's practice; one of much importance in the evolution of his art. "Sidonia von Bork" was one of the characters in a romance called "Sidonia the Sorceress," which was written by a Swiss clergyman. The book was a favourite of Rossetti's, so that evidently Burne-Jones was influenced by his master both in his choice and in his treatment of a subject from its pages. A reprint of the story was issued by William Morris from the Kelmscott Press.

SPONSA DI LIBANO
(Walker Art Gallery, Liverpool)

The first idea for the "Sponsa di Libano" was embodied in one of a series of pencil designs from the "Song of Solomon," which were prepared by Burne-Jones in 1876. This picture, the only one out of the series which he actually completed pictorially, was exhibited at the New Gallery in 1891. The motive of the composition is explained in the text which the original drawing illustrated: "Awake, O North Wind; and come, thou South; blow upon my garden that the spices thereof may flow out." In the treatment of the subject the artist's poetic fancy and sense of decorative arrangement are particularly well displayed.

SIBYLLA DELPHICA
(Manchester Art Gallery)

In this painting of the Delphic oracle Burne-Jones made no attempt to reconstruct archæologically an incident from classic times. The symbolism of the subject appealed to him rather than its possibilities of being represented realistically, and he treated it in a manner entirely personal, with strength and decision, but with exquisite tenderness of poetic sentiment as well. The picture has a certain intensity of feeling that is especially convincing, and its fine draughtsmanship, splendid colour, and well-considered suggestion of movement make it technically of very great importance.

THE MILL
(South Kensington Museum)

This picture is one of those on which Burne-Jones worked at intervals for several years. Commenced in 1870, and taken up and set aside time after time, it was not exhibited until 1882, when it appeared at the Grosvenor Gallery. It is an example, and a very attractive one, of the daintier side of the artist's practice, a decorative composition planned with masterly restraint and with a wholly sympathetic understanding of the charm of pure and unforced sentiment. It has both grace and distinction.

KING COPHETUA AND THE BEGGAR MAID
(The Tate Gallery)

The old story of the king who succumbed to the charms of a simple beggar maid has inspired many artists, but none have rivalled Burne-Jones in appreciation of the artistic possibilities of the subject. His picture on its appearance at the Grosvenor Gallery in 1884 set the seal on his reputation, and put an end to whatever doubts remained then in the public mind as to his right to serious consideration. It is in many ways the finest of all his works, the most ambitious and the most exacting in the technical problems presented, and it is certainly the most notable in accomplishment.

DANAE (The Tower of Brass)
(Glasgow Corporation Art Gallery)

Like the "Sibylla Delphica" this canvas shows how Burne-Jones was accustomed to treat subjects from the classic myths in the mediæval spirit to which he inclined by habit and association. In his illustration of a subject from the story of Danae, where she stands watching in wonder the building of the tower of brass which was to be her prison, he has looked at Greek tradition in a way that was partly his own and partly a reflection of William Morris; but the result is none the less persuasive because it does not conform to the Greek convention.

THE ENCHANTMENTS OF NIMUE
(South Kensington Museum)

Painted, like the "Sidonia von Bork," while Burne-Jones was still under the influence of Rossetti, "The Enchantments of Nimue" is interesting as an example of his earliest methods. It was finished in 1861, but it was not exhibited until 1865, when it was hung in the Gallery of the Royal Society of Painters in Water Colours; it was bought for the South Kensington Museum in 1896. The painting shows how Nimue "caused Merlin to pass under a heaving-stone into a grave" by the power of her enchantments

On the following pages are some contemporaries of Burne-Jones.

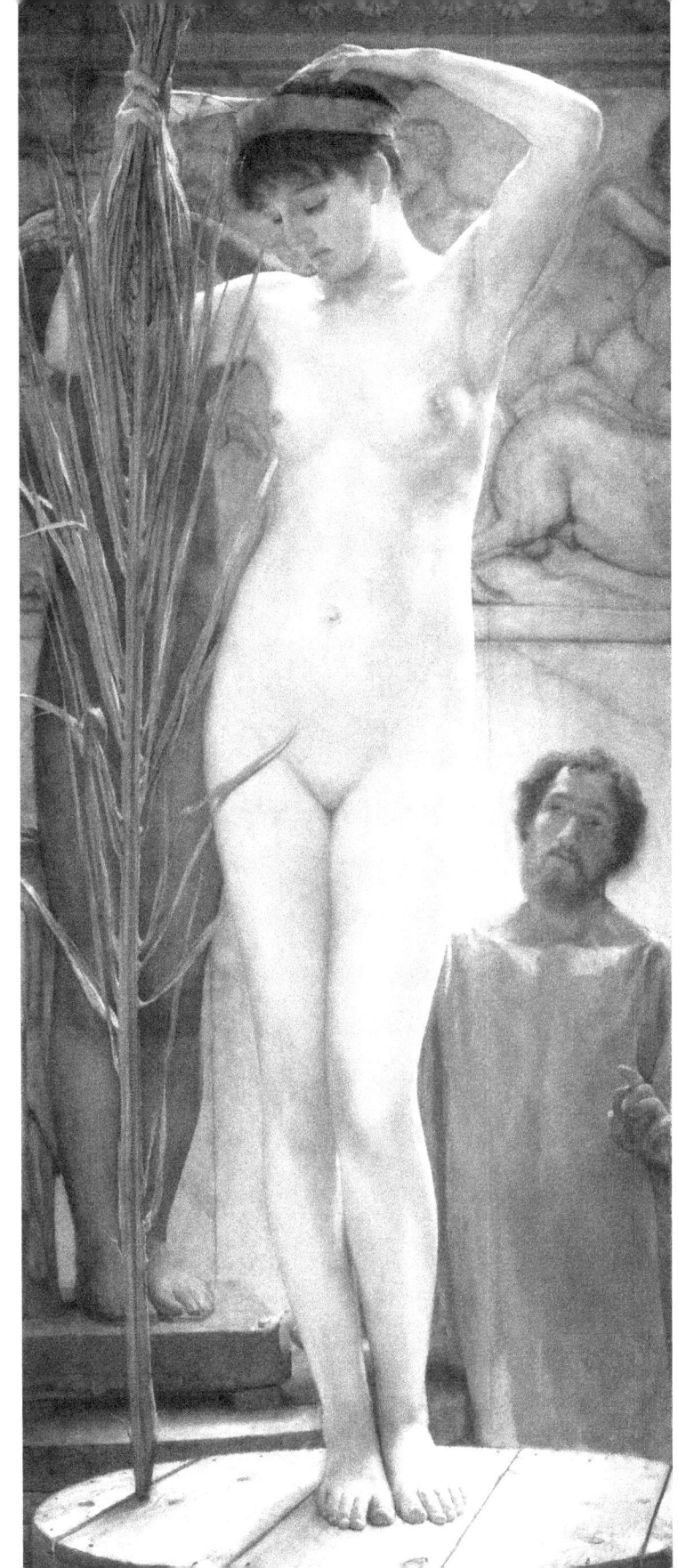

Lawrence
Alma-Tadema,
A Sculptor's Model,
1877, private
collection

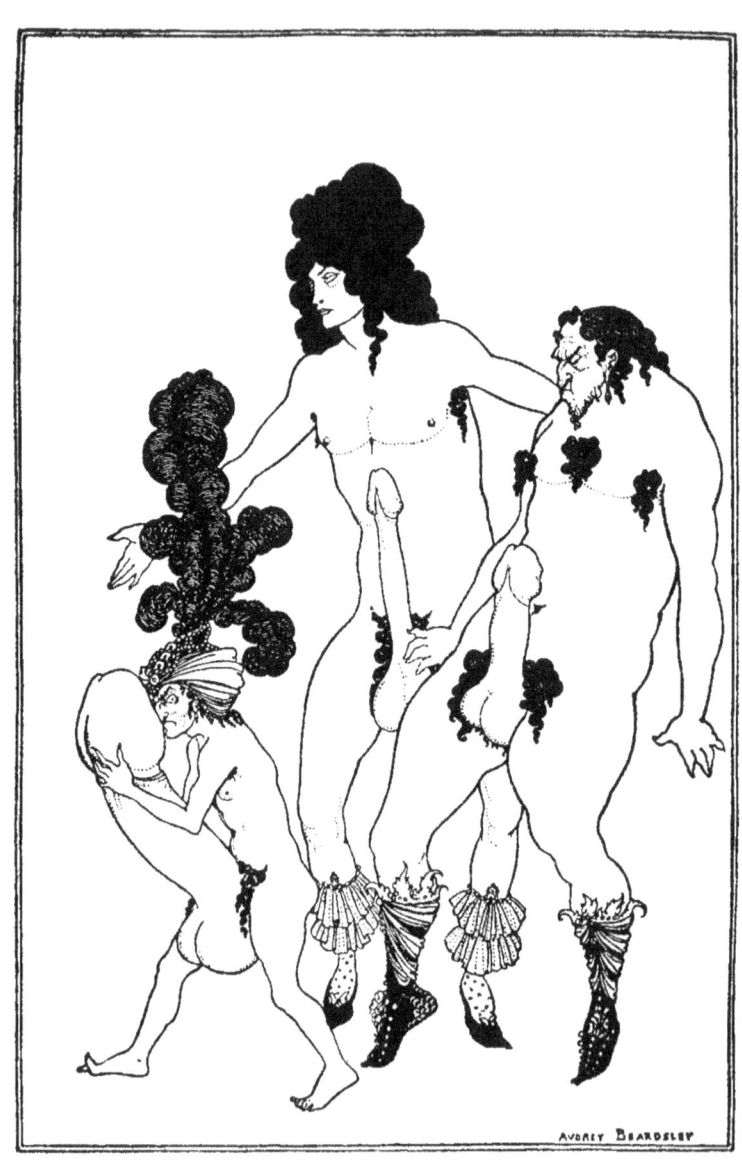

Aubrey Beardsley, Aristophanes, Lysistrata, 1896

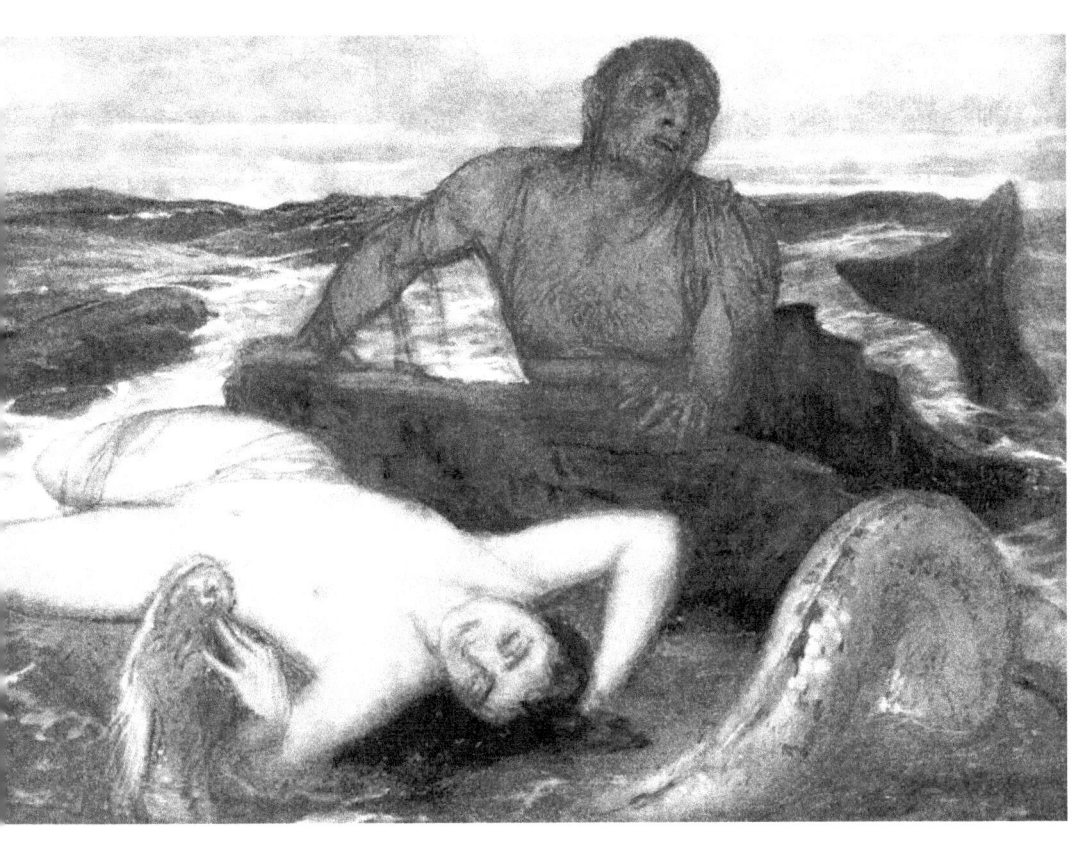

Arnold Böcklin, Triton and Nereid, 1877

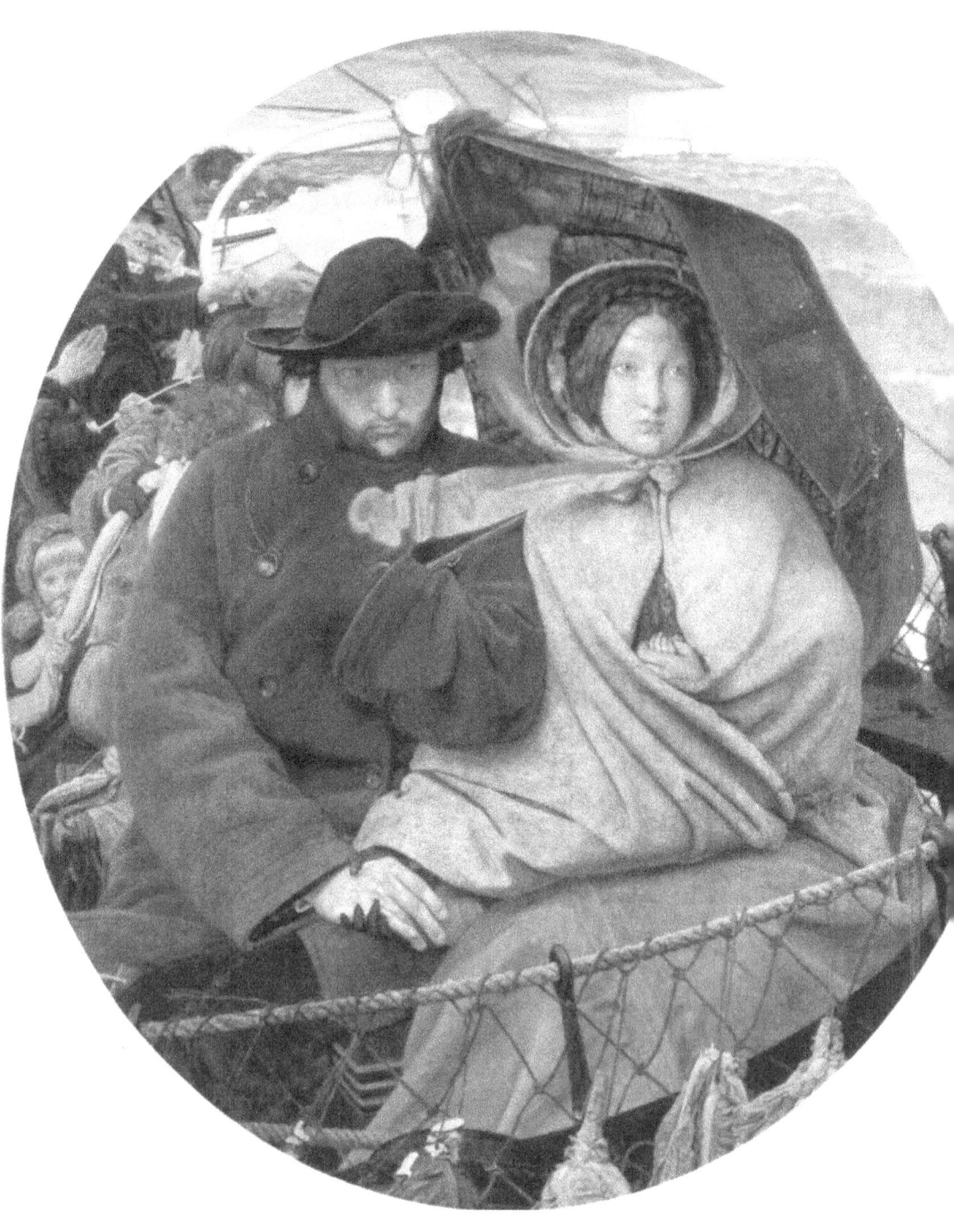

Ford Madox Brown, The Last of England, 1855,
Birmingham

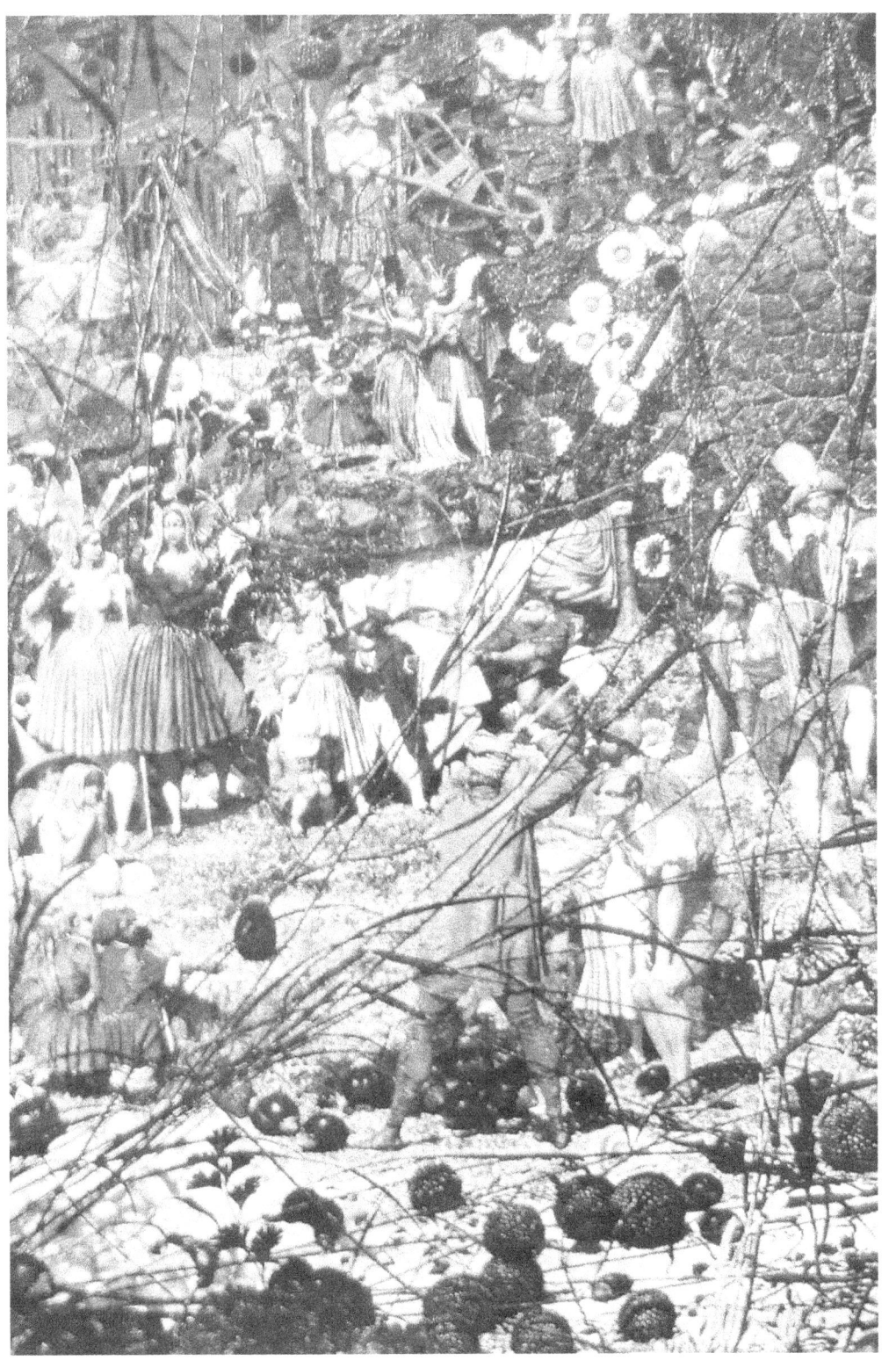

Richard Dadd, The Fairy-Feller's Master-Stroke, Tate, London

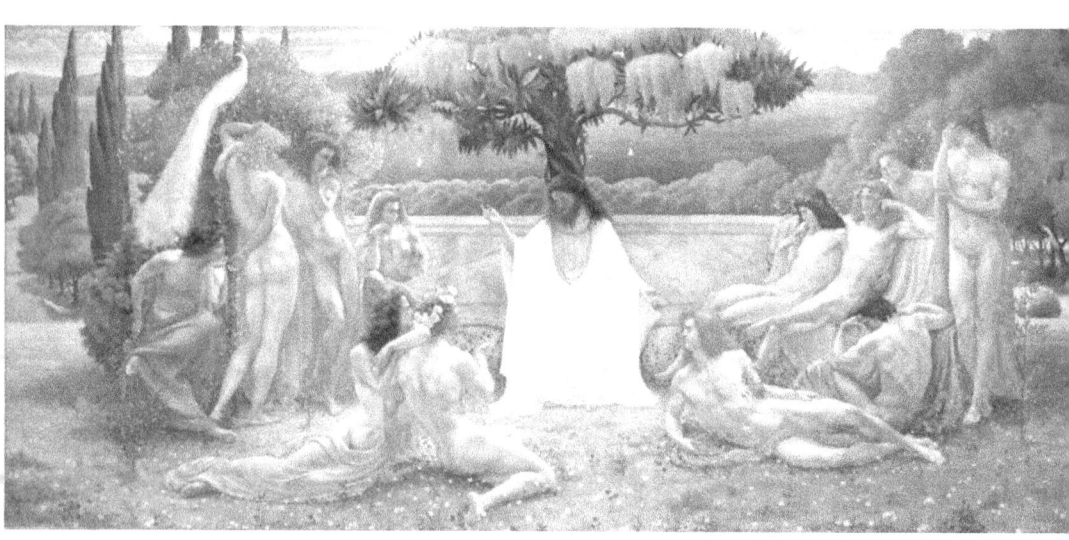

Jean Delville, The School of Plato, 1898

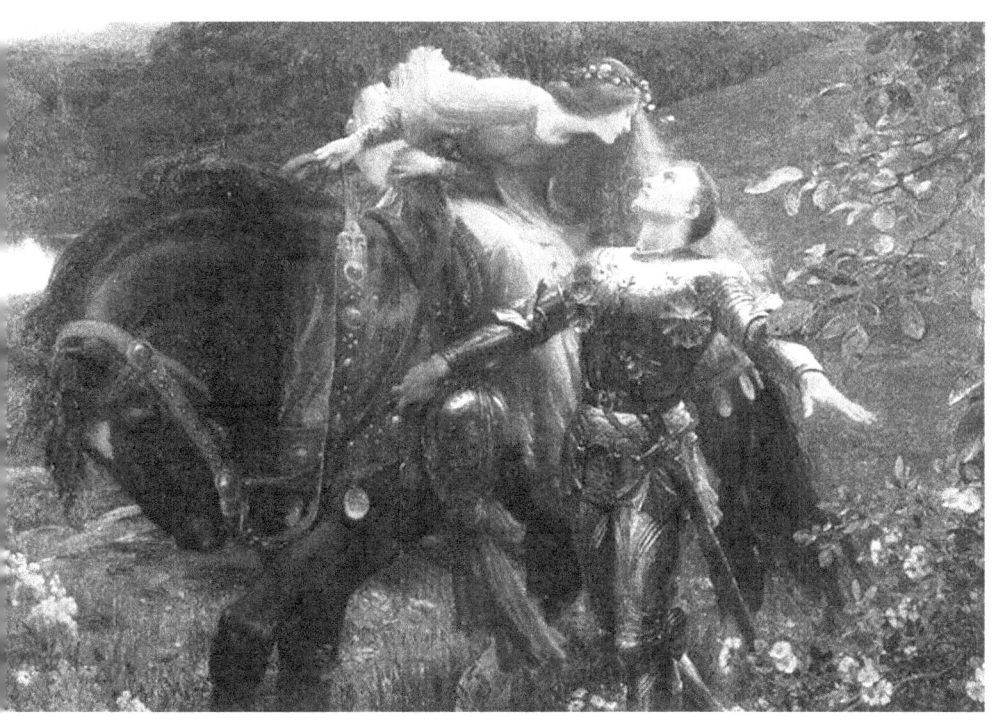

Sir Francis Dicksee, 'La Belle Dame Sans Merci'

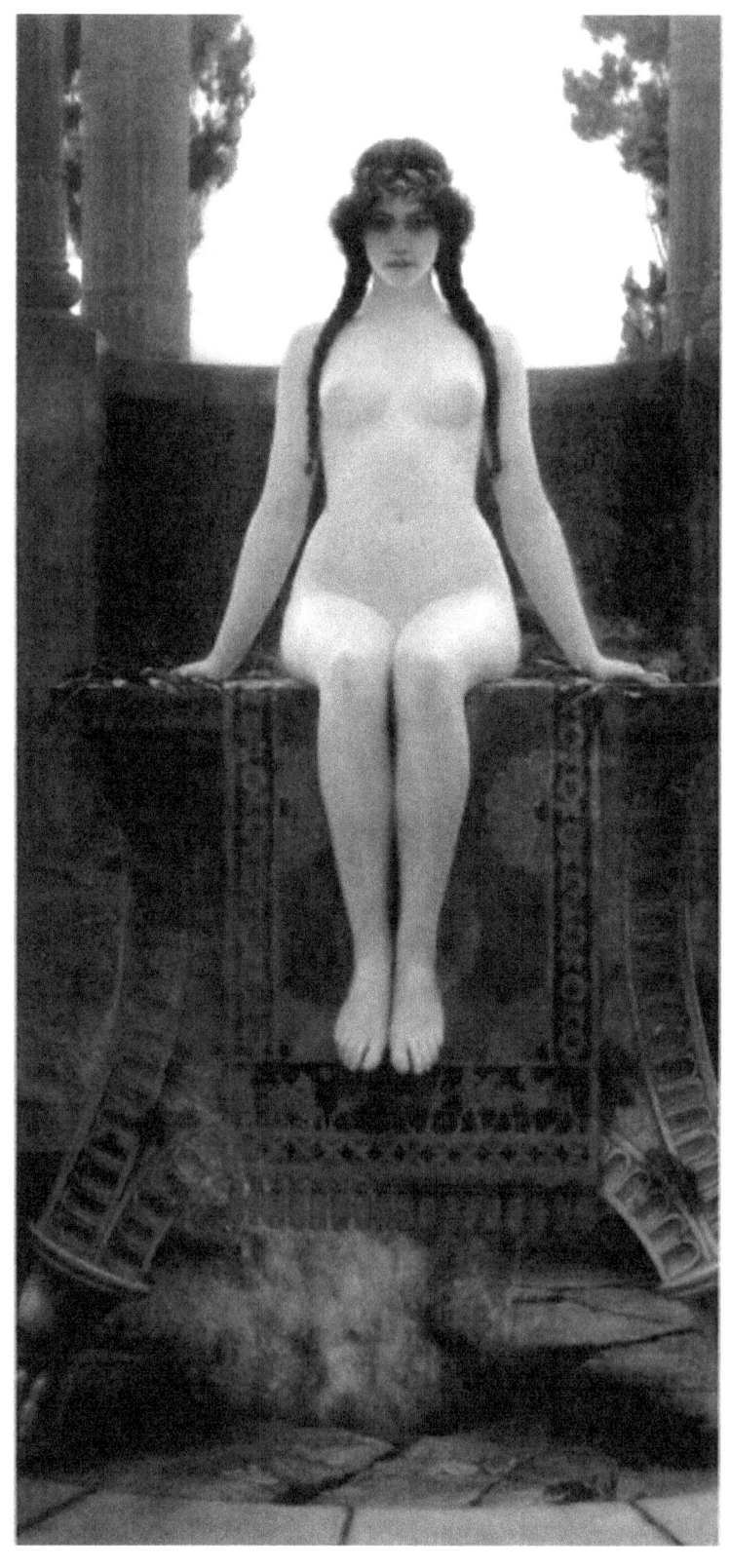

John Godward, The Delphic Oracle, 1899

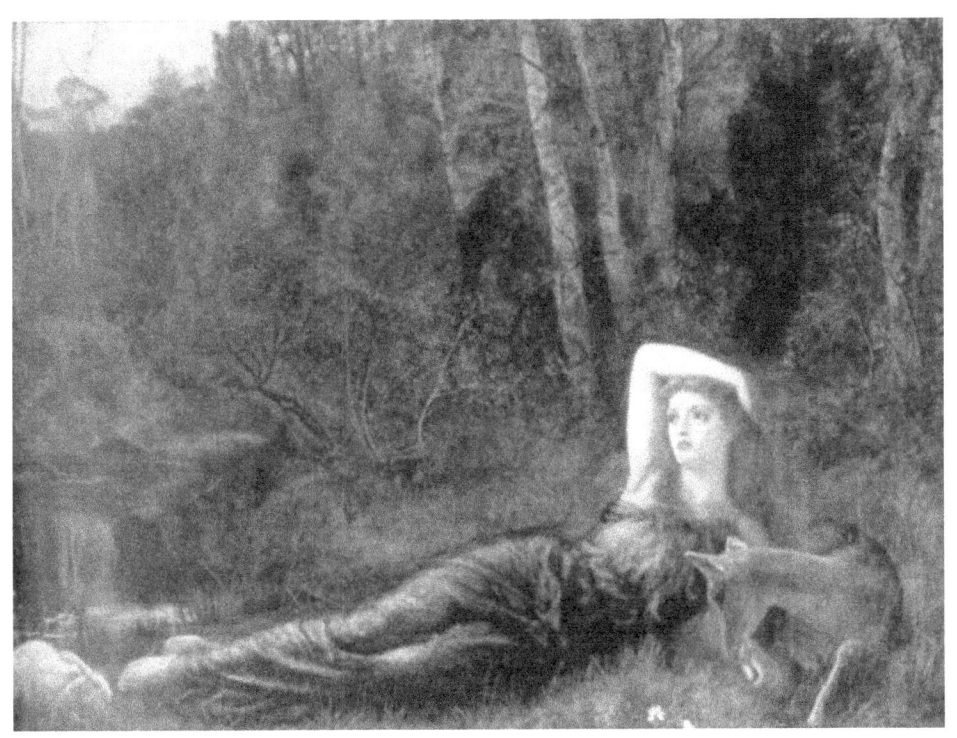

Arthur Hughes, Endymion

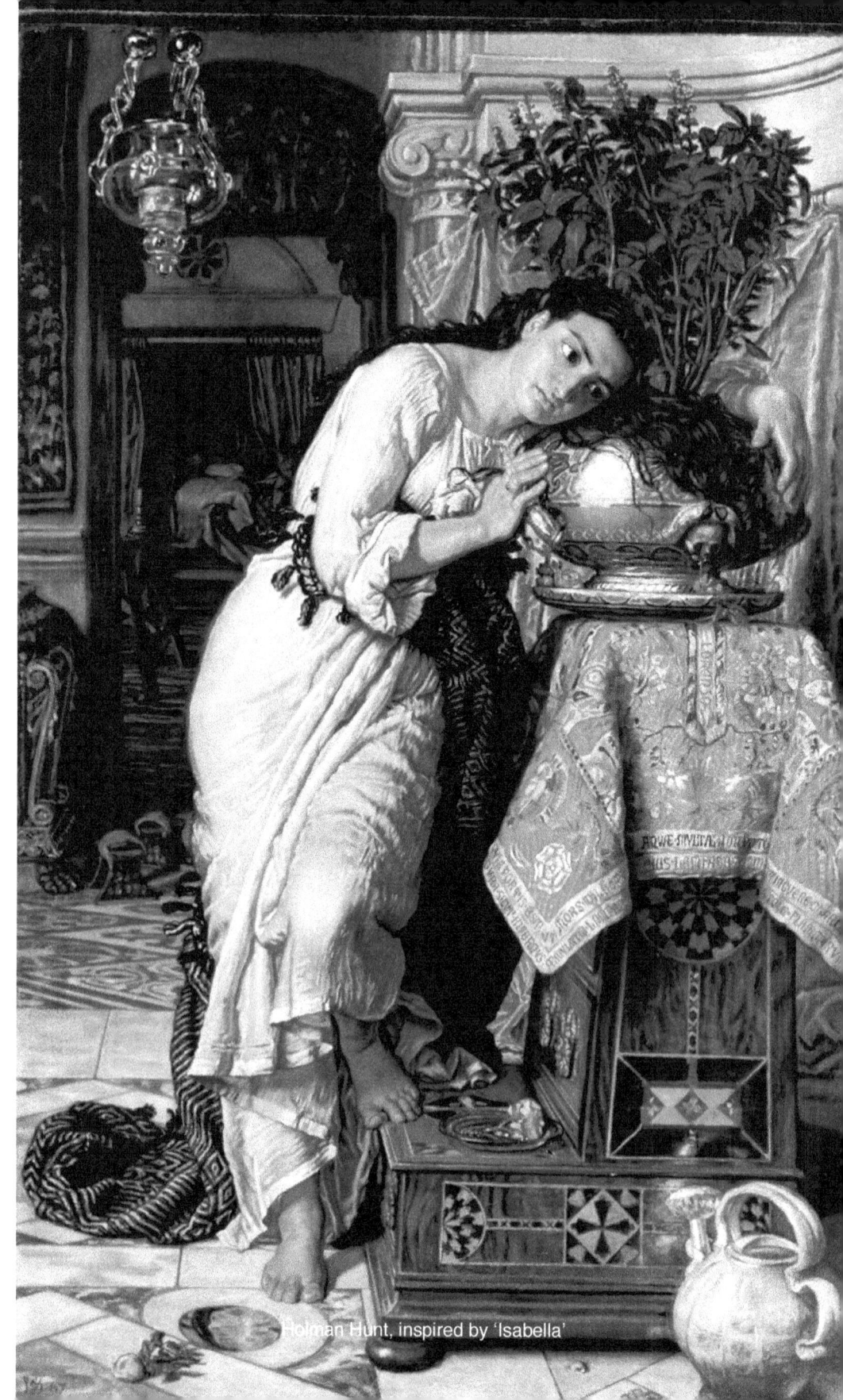

Holman Hunt, inspired by 'Isabella'

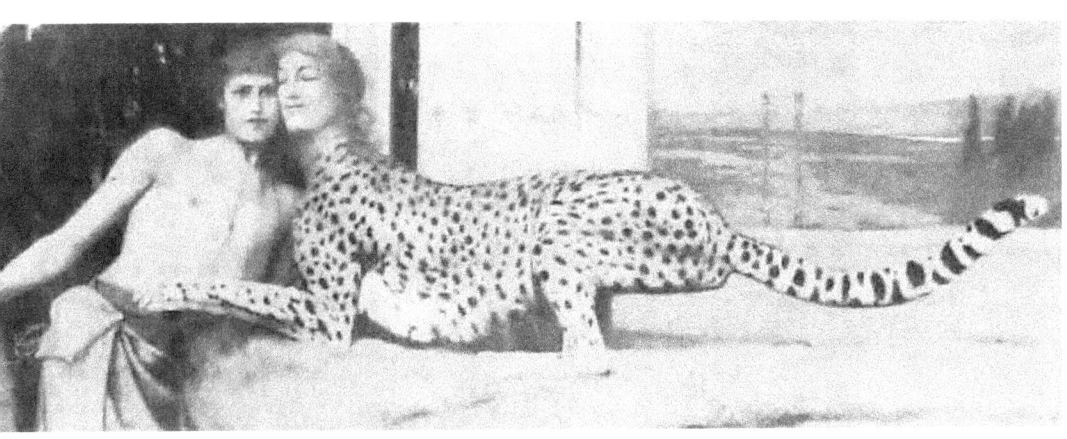

Fernand Knopff, The Caresses of the Sphinx, 1896, Brussels

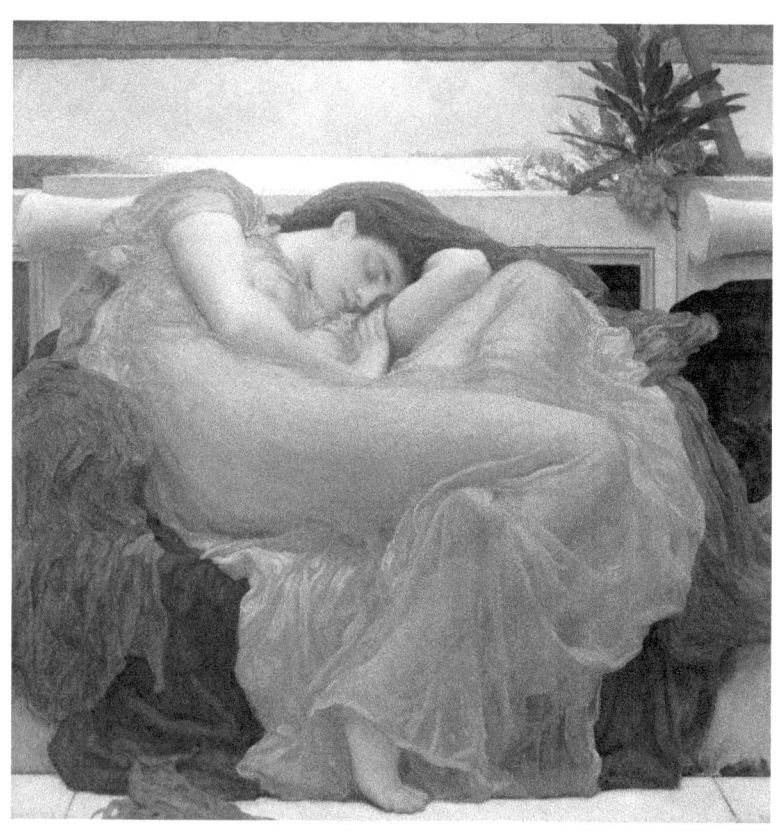

Lord Leighton, Flaming June, 1895, Puerto Rico

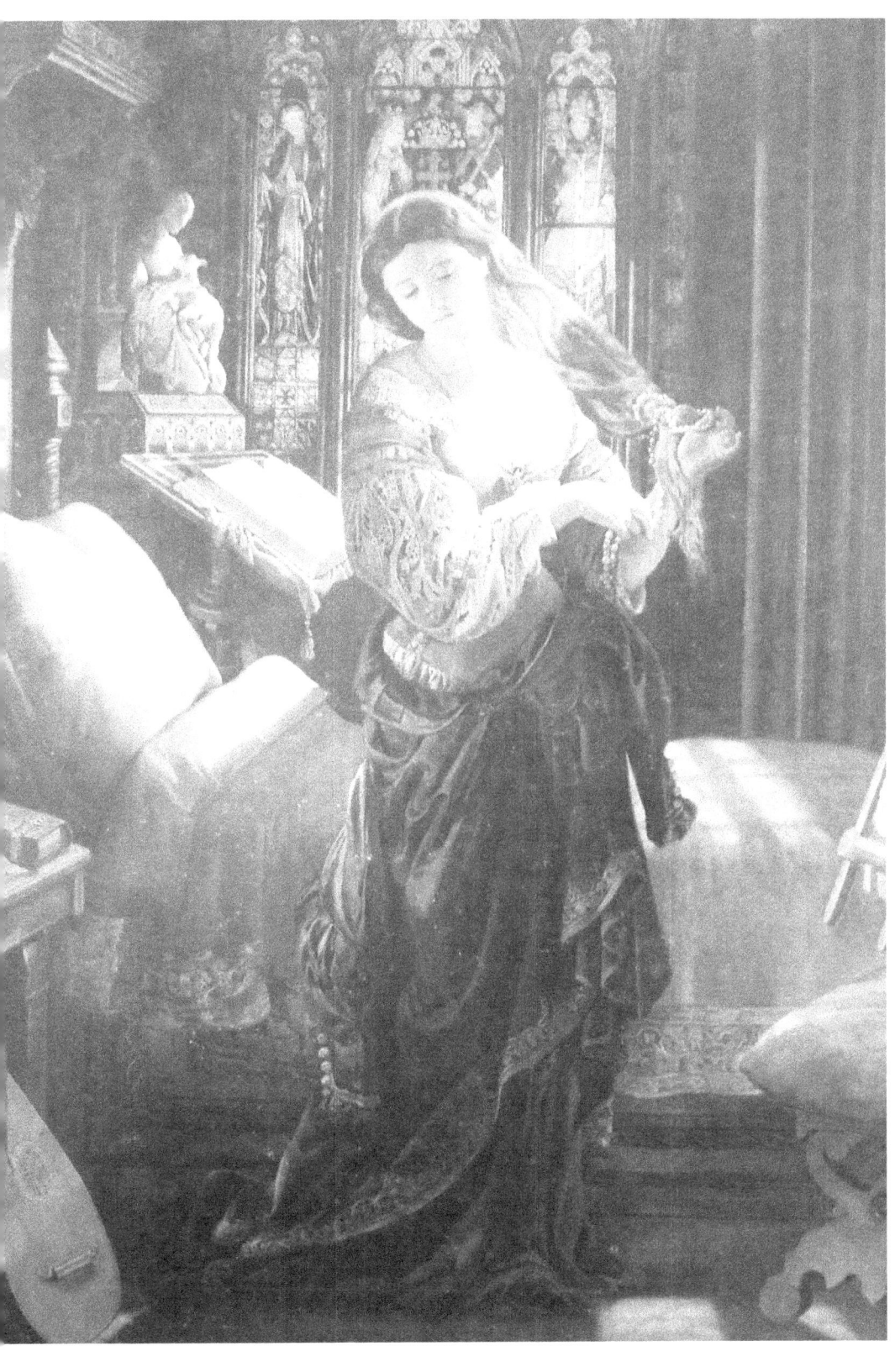

Daniel Maclise, Madeline After Prayer, 1868, Walker Art Gallery

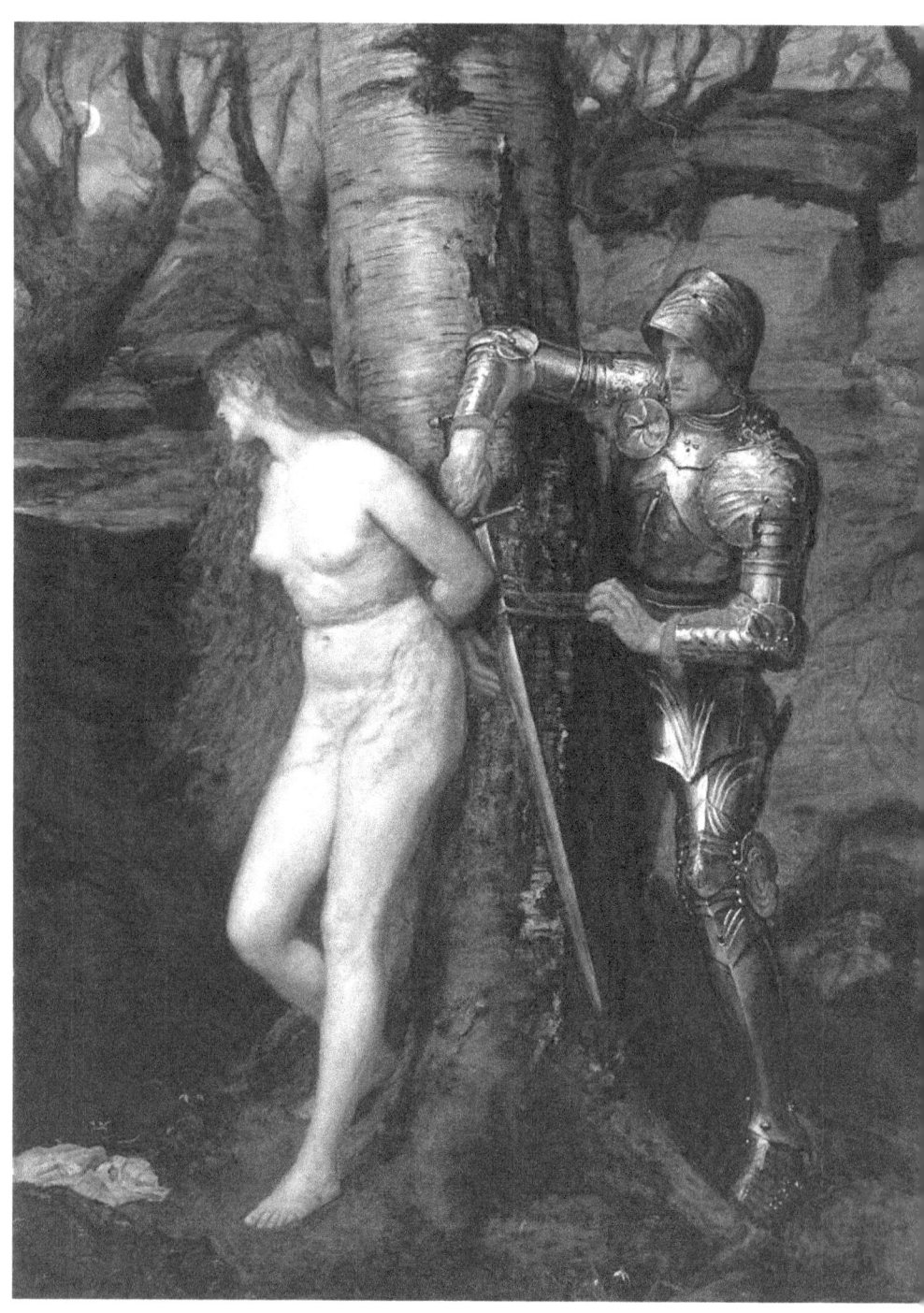

John Everett Millais, The Knight Errant, 1870, Tate, London

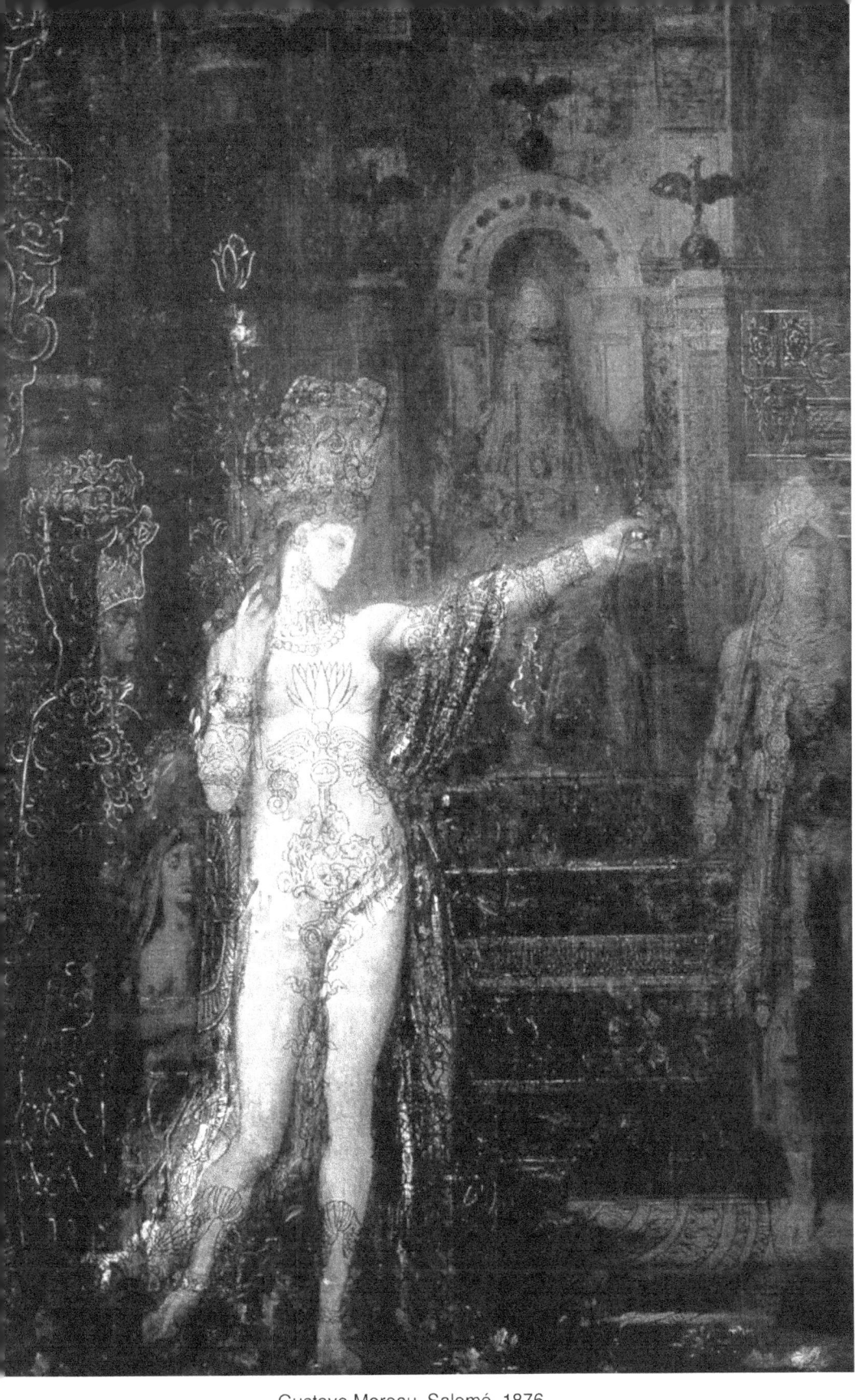

Gustave Moreau, Salomé, 1876

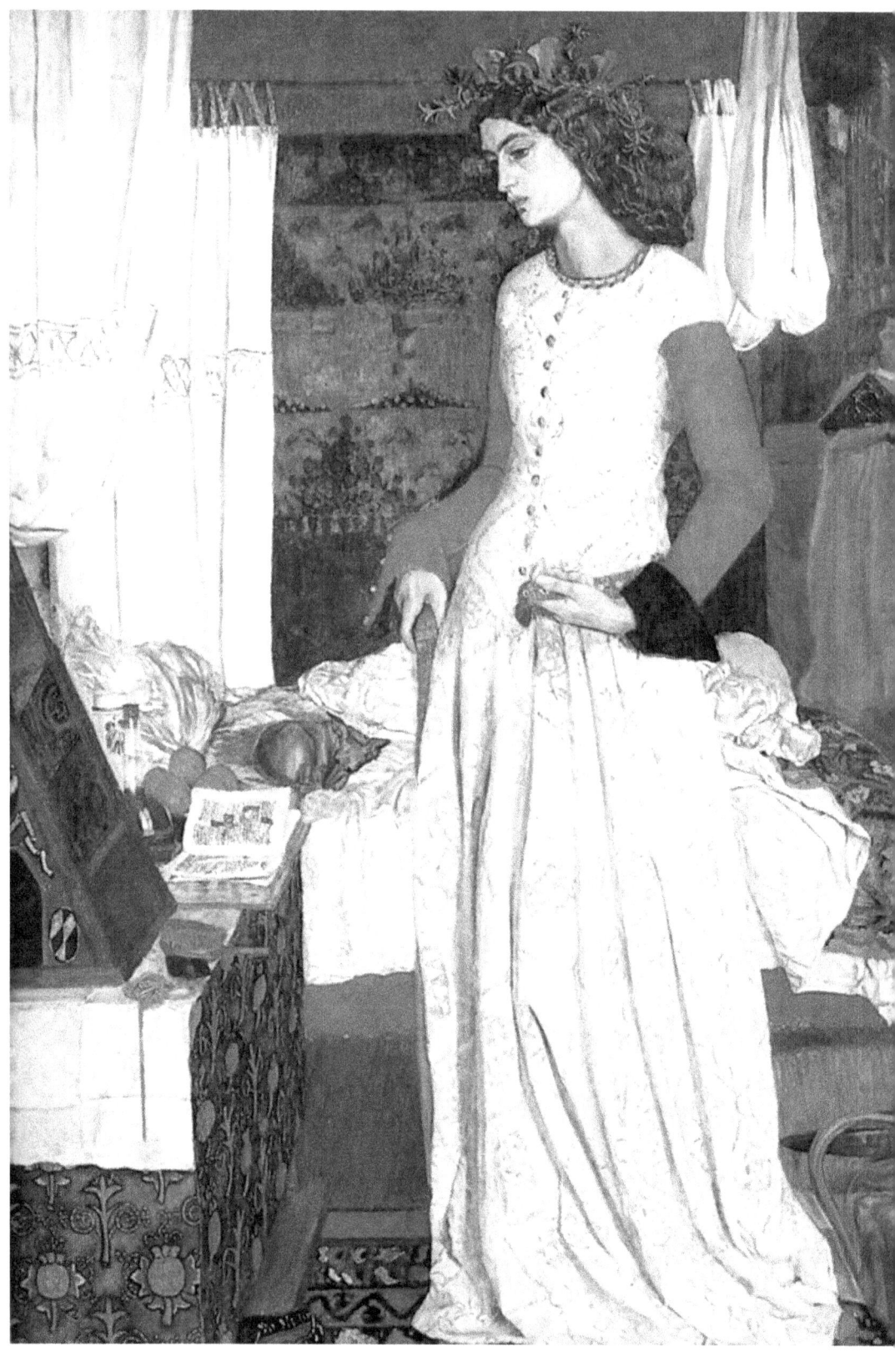

William Morris, La Belle Iseult, 1858, Tate Gallery

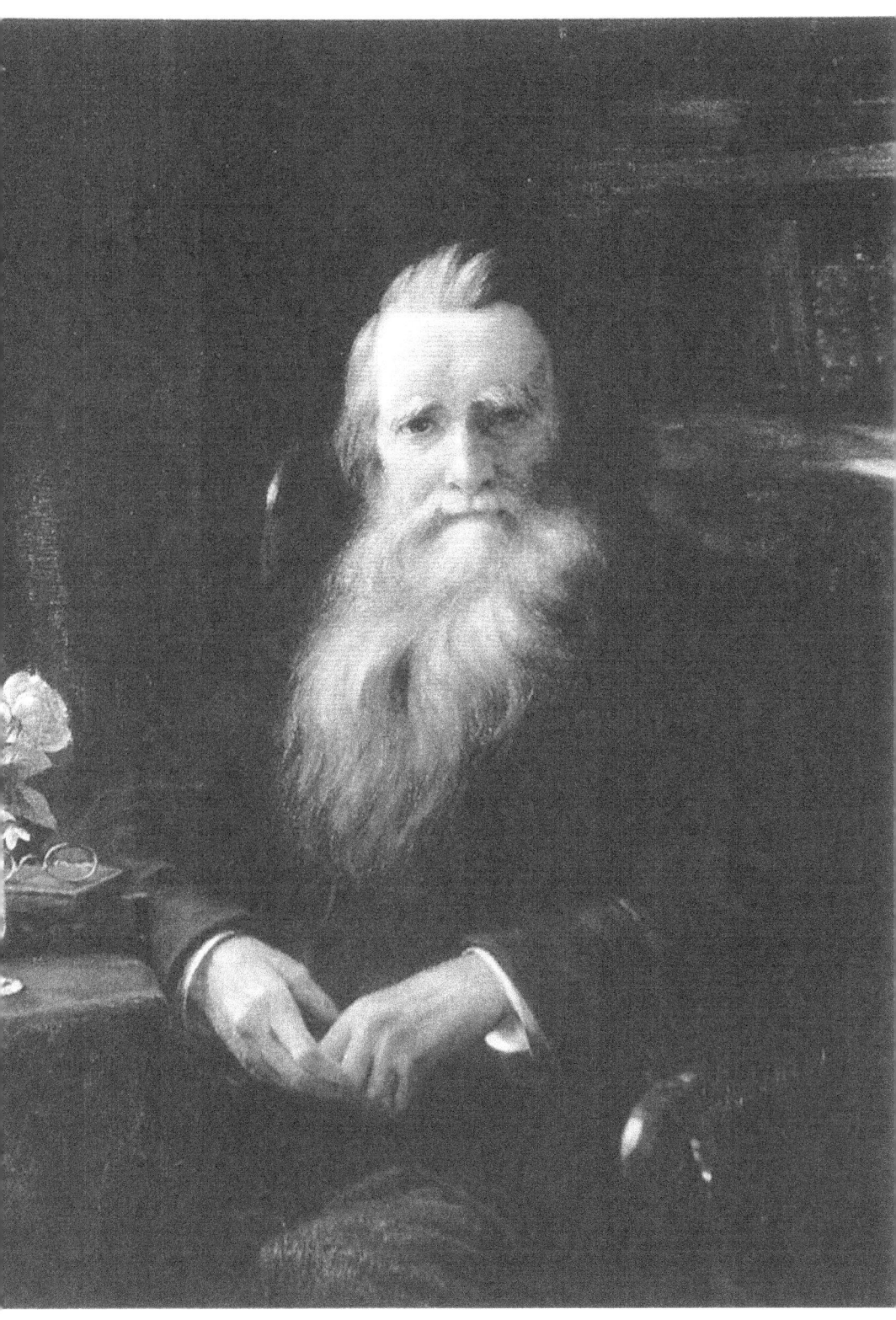

W.G. Collingwood,John Ruskin, 1897

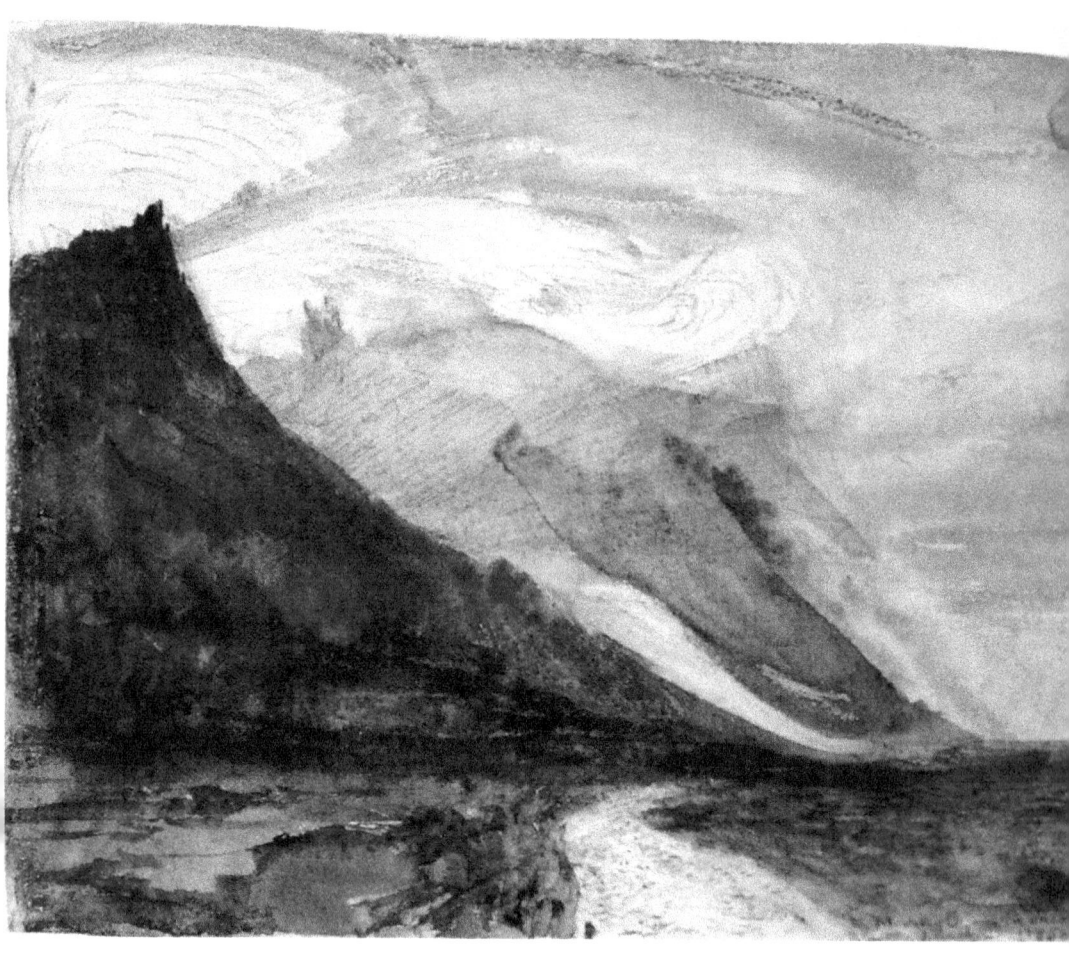

John Ruskin, Moonlight, Chamonix, 1888

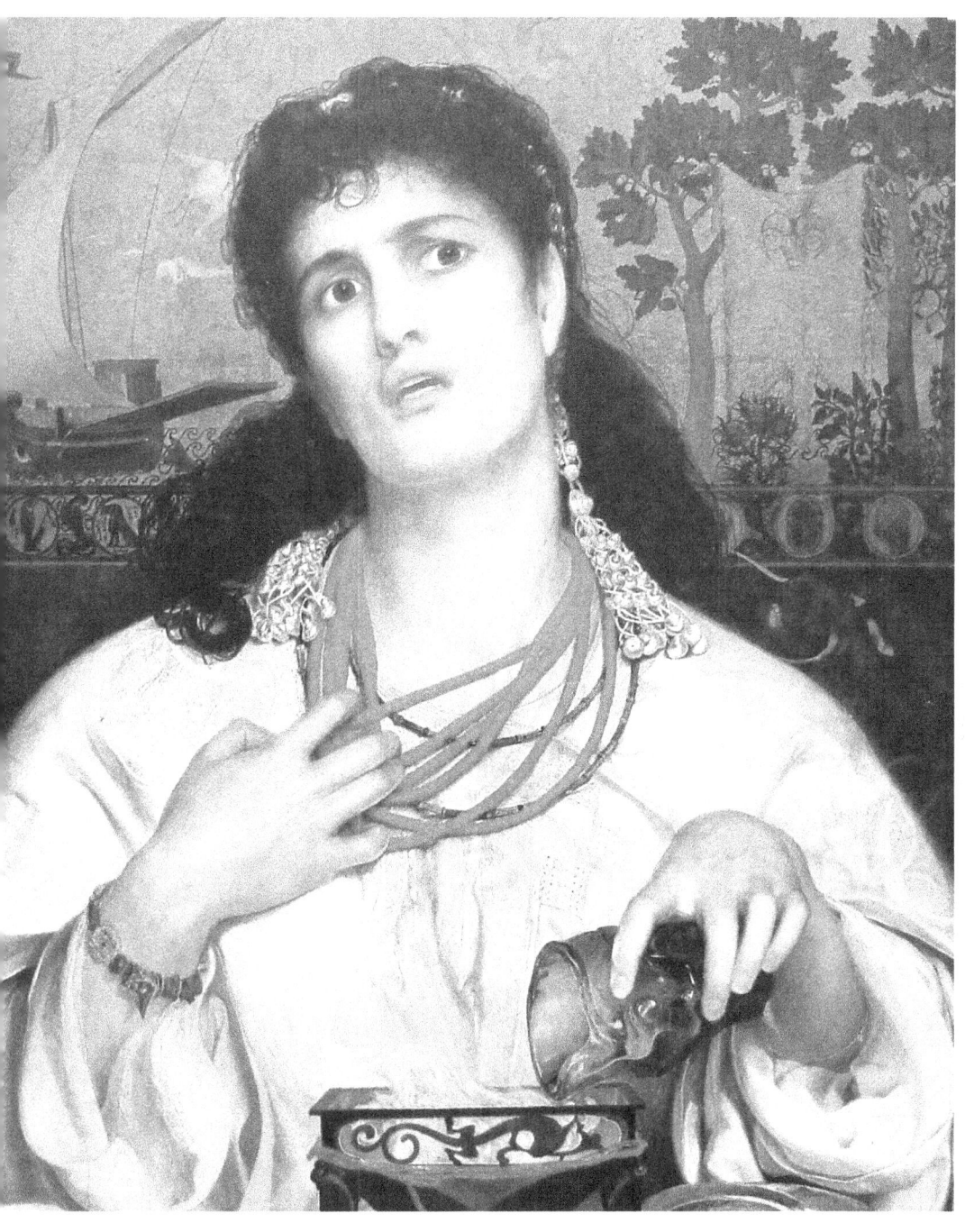

Frederick Sandys, Medea, 1868

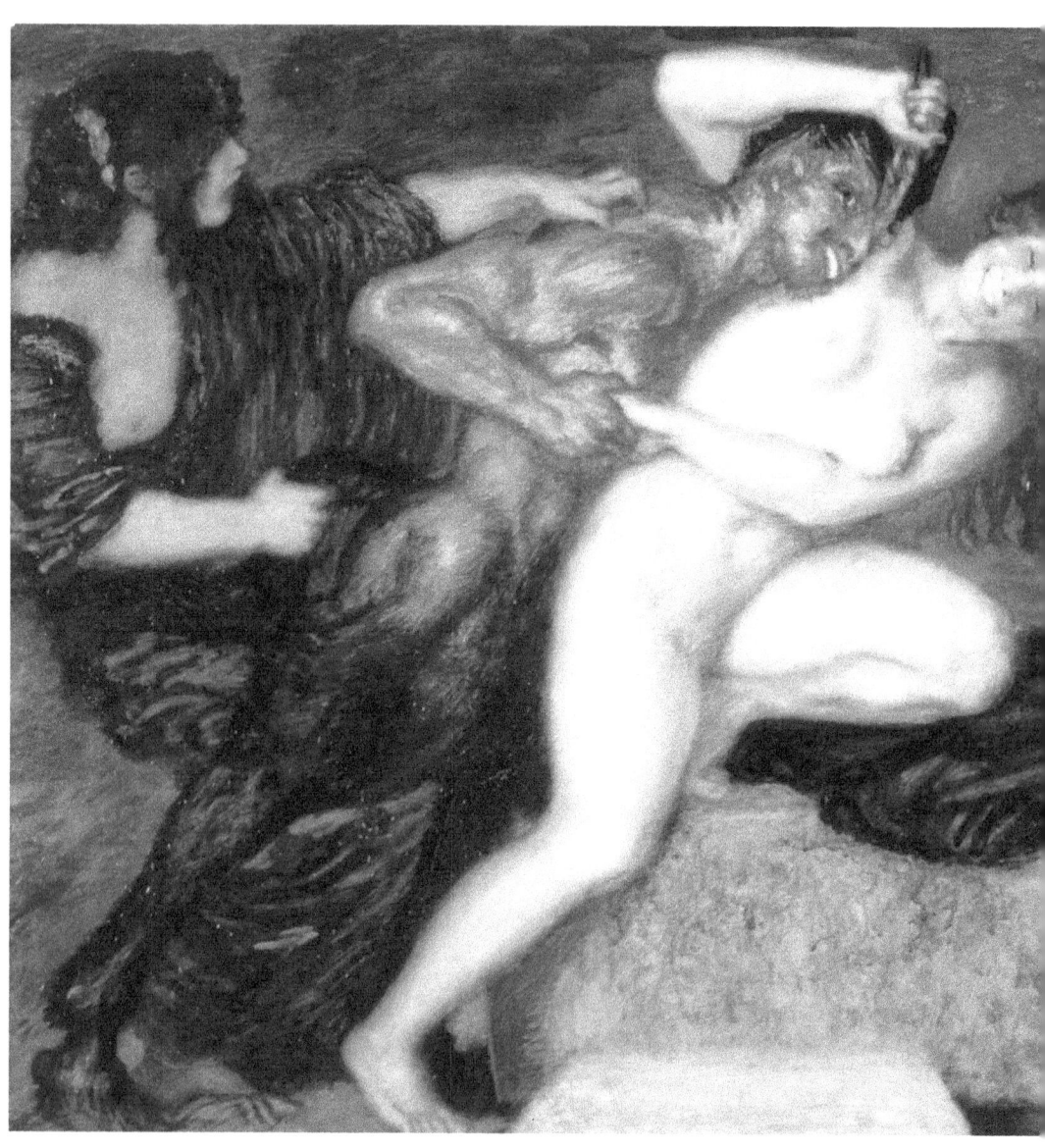

Franz von Stuck, Scherzo

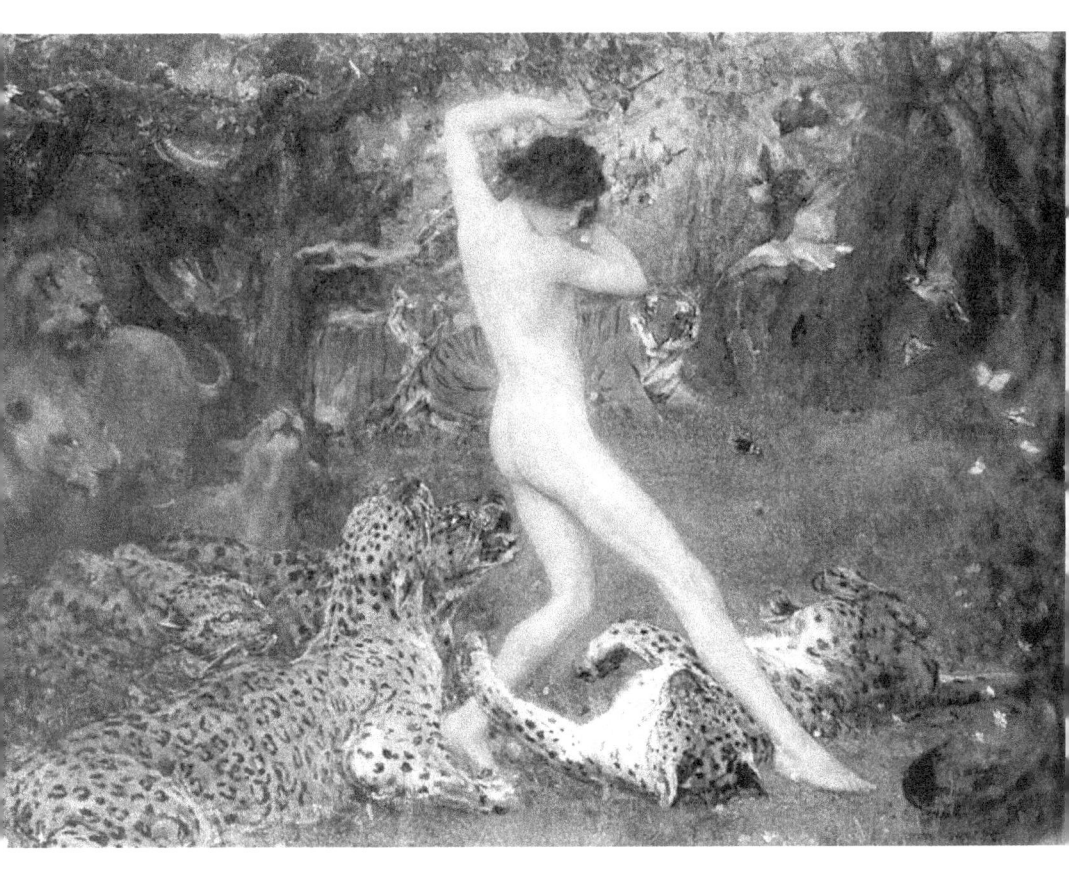

John Macallan Swan, Orpheus, 1896

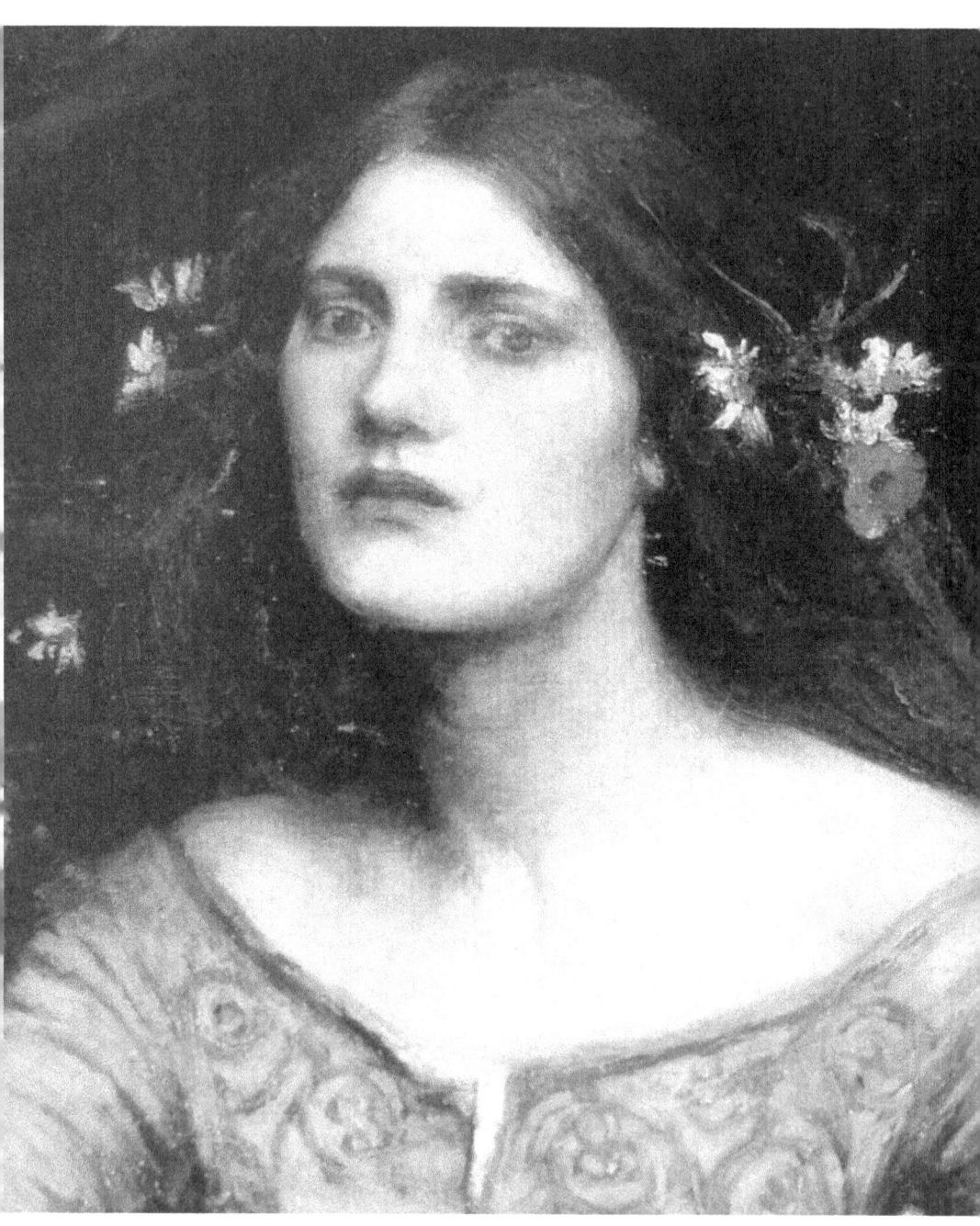

John William Waterhouse, Ophelia, 1910, detail

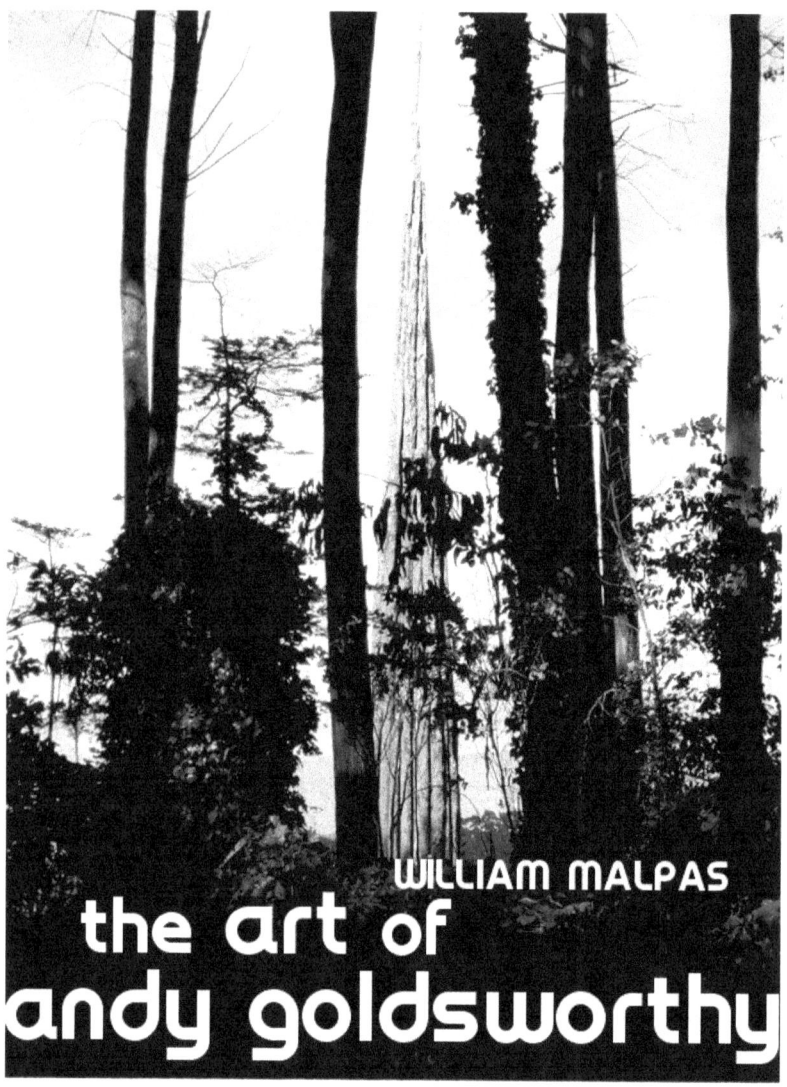

WILLIAM MALPAS
the art of
andy goldsworthy

This is the most comprehensive and detailed account of the art of Andy Goldsworthy available.

This study of Andy Goldsworthy discusses all of Goldsworthy's major exhibitions, books and projects, including the *Sheepfolds* project; *Garden of Stones* in New York; TV and dance collaborations; and the books *Wood, Stone, Time* and *Passage*. William Malpas surveys all of Goldsworthy's output, and analyzes his relation with other land artists such as Robert Smithson, the Christos, Walter de Maria, Chris Drury, Richard Long and David Nash; women sculptors; sculpture in the modern era; and Goldsworthy's place in the contemporary British art scene.

The book has been updated and revised for this new edition.

ISBN 9781861714107 Pbk   ISBN 9781861714114 Hbk
Fully illustrated   www.crmoon.com

MAURICE SENDAK

& the art of children's book illustration

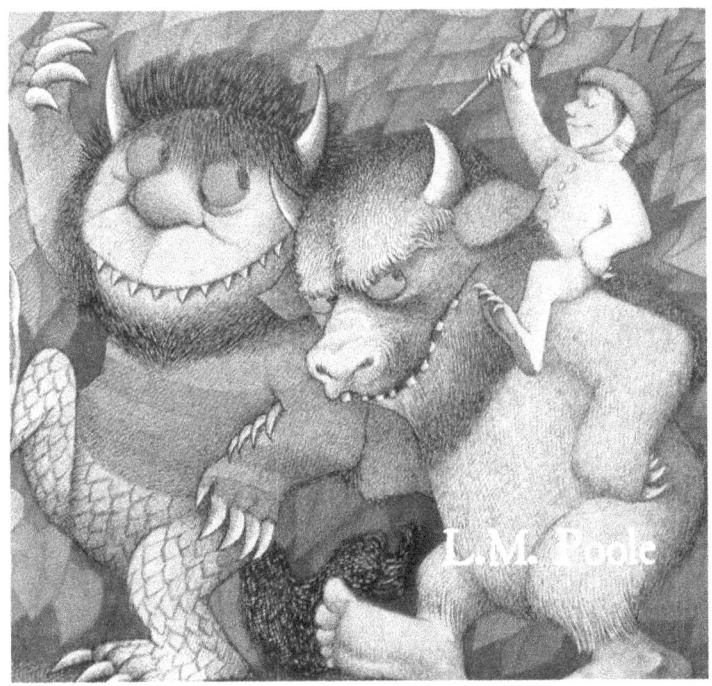

Maurice Sendak is the widely acclaimed American children's book author and illustrator. This critical study focuses on his famous trilogy, *Where the Wild Things Are, In the Night Kitchen* and *Outside Over There*, as well as the early works and Sendak's superb depictions of the Grimm Brothers' fairy tales in *The Juniper Tree*. L.M. Poole begins with a chapter on children's book illustration, in particular the treatment of fairy tales. Sendak's work is situated within the history of children's book illustration, and he is compared with many contemporary authors.

Fully illustrated. The book has been revised and updated for this edition.
ISBN 9781861714282 Pbk   ISBN 9781861713469 Hbk

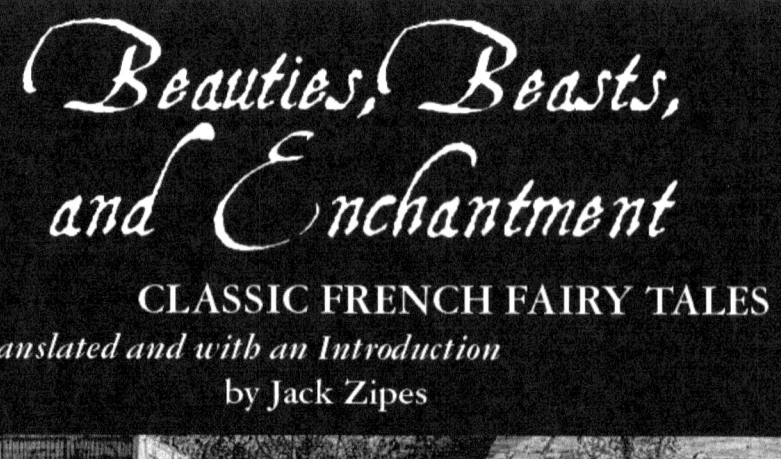

Beauties, Beasts, and Enchantment

CLASSIC FRENCH FAIRY TALES

Translated and with an Introduction
by Jack Zipes

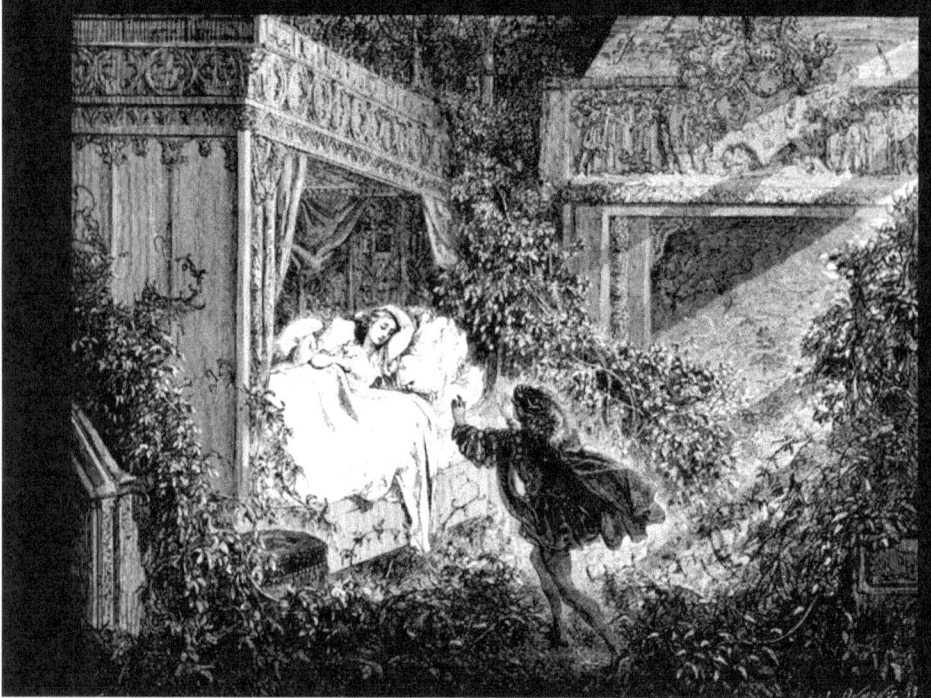

A collection of 36 classic French fairy tales translated by renowned writer Jack Zipes. *Cinderella, Beauty and the Beast, Sleeping Beauty* and *Little Red Riding Hood* are among the classic fairy tales in this amazing book.
Includes illustrations from fairy tale collections.
Jack Zipes has written and published widely on fairy tales.

'Terrific... a succulent array of 17th and 18th century 'salon' fairy tales'
- *The New York Times Book Review*

'These tales are adventurous, thrilling in a way fairy tales are meant to be... The translation from the French is modern, happily free of archaic and hyperbolic language... a fine and sophisticated collection' - *New York Tribune*

'Enjoyable to read... a unique collection of French regional folklore' - *Library Journal*

'Charming stories accompanied by attractive pen-and-ink drawings' - *Chattanooga Times*

Introduction and illustrations   612pp.   ISBN 9781861712510 Pbk   ISBN 9781861713193 Hbk

CRESCENT MOON PUBLISHING

web: www.crmoon.com e-mail: cresmopub@yahoo.co.uk

ARTS, PAINTING, SCULPTURE

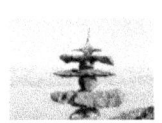
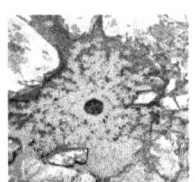

The Art of Andy Goldsworthy
Andy Goldsworthy: Touching Nature
Andy Goldsworthy in Close-Up
Andy Goldsworthy: Pocket Guide
Andy Goldsworthy In America
Land Art: A Complete Guide
The Art of Richard Long

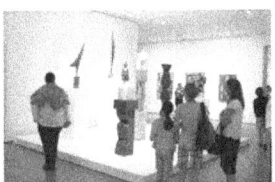
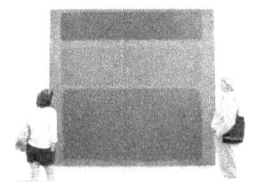

Richard Long: Pocket Guide
Land Art In the UK
Land Art in Close-Up
Land Art In the U.S.A.
Land Art: Pocket Guide
Installation Art in Close-Up
Minimal Art and Artists In the 1960s and After
Colourfield Painting
Land Art DVD, TV documentary
Andy Goldsworthy DVD, TV documentary
The Erotic Object: Sexuality in Sculpture From Prehistory to the Present Day

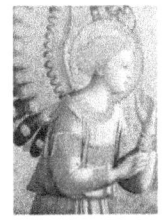

Sex in Art: Pornography and Pleasure in Painting and Sculpture
Postwar Art
Sacred Gardens: The Garden in Myth, Religion and Art
Glorification: Religious Abstraction in Renaissance and 20th Century Art
Early Netherlandish Painting
Leonardo da Vinci
Piero della Francesca
Giovanni Bellini

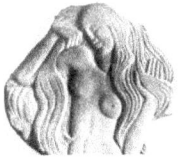
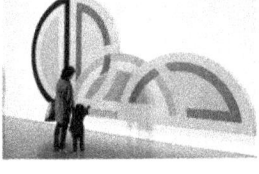

Fra Angelico: Art and Religion in the Renaissance
Mark Rothko: The Art of Transcendence
Frank Stella: American Abstract Artist
Jasper Johns
Brice Marden

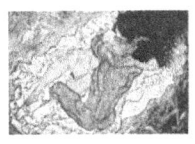
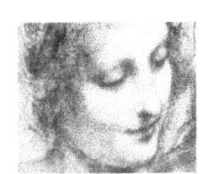

Alison Wilding: The Embrace of Sculpture
Vincent van Gogh: Visionary Landscapes
Eric Gill: Nuptials of God
Constantin Brancusi: Sculpting the Essence of Things
Max Beckmann
Caravaggio
Gustave Moreau
Egon Schiele: Sex and Death In Purple Stockings
Delizioso Fotografico Fervore: Works In Process 1
Sacro Cuore: Works In Process 2

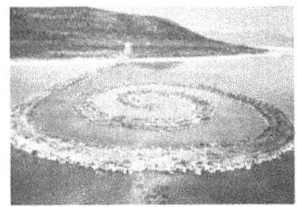

The Light Eternal: J.M.W. Turner
The Madonna Glorified: Karen Arthurs

LITERATURE

J.R.R. Tolkien: The Books, The Films, The Whole Cultural Phenomenon
J.R.R. Tolkien: Pocket Guide
Tolkien's Heroic Quest
The *Earthsea* Books of Ursula Le Guin
Beauties, Beasts and Enchantment: Classic French Fairy Tales
German Popular Stories by the Brothers Grimm
Philip Pullman and *His Dark Materials*
Sexing Hardy: Thomas Hardy and Feminism
Thomas Hardy's *Tess of the d'Urbervilles*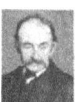
Thomas Hardy's *Jude the Obscure*
Thomas Hardy: The Tragic Novels
Love and Tragedy: Thomas Hardy
The Poetry of Landscape in Hardy
Wessex Revisited: Thomas Hardy and John Cowper Powys
Wolfgang Iser: Essays and Interviews
Petrarch, Dante and the Troubadours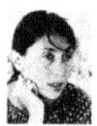
Maurice Sendak and the Art of Children's Book Illustration
Andrea Dworkin
Cixous, Irigaray, Kristeva: The *Jouissance* of French Feminism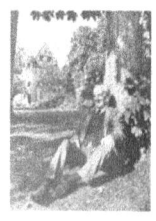
Julia Kristeva: Art, Love, Melancholy, Philosophy, Semiotics and Psychoanalysis
Hélene Cixous I Love You: The *Jouissance* of Writing
Luce Irigaray: Lips, Kissing, and the Politics of Sexual Difference
Peter Redgrove: Here Comes the Flood
Peter Redgrove: Sex-Magic-Poetry-Cornwall
Lawrence Durrell: Between Love and Death, East and West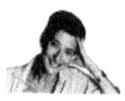
Love, Culture & Poetry: Lawrence Durrell
Cavafy: Anatomy of a Soul
German Romantic Poetry: Goethe, Novalis, Heine, Hölderlin
Feminism and Shakespeare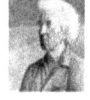
Shakespeare: Love, Poetry & Magic
The Passion of D.H. Lawrence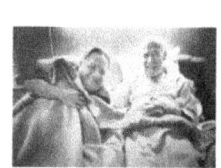
D.H. Lawrence: Symbolic Landscapes
D.H. Lawrence: Infinite Sensual Violence
Rimbaud: Arthur Rimbaud and the Magic of Poetry
The Ecstasies of John Cowper Powys
Sensualism and Mythology: The Wessex Novels of John Cowper Powys
Amorous Life: John Cowper Powys and the Manifestation of Affectivity (H.W. Fawkner)
Postmodern Powys: New Essays on John Cowper Powys (Joe Boulter)
Rethinking Powys: Critical Essays on John Cowper Powys
Paul Bowles & Bernardo Bertolucci
Rainer Maria Rilke
Joseph Conrad: *Heart of Darkness*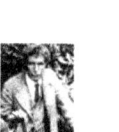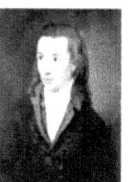
In the Dim Void: Samuel Beckett
Samuel Beckett Goes into the Silence
André Gide: Fiction and Fervour
Jackie Collins and the Blockbuster Novel
Blinded By Her Light: The Love-Poetry of Robert Graves
The Passion of Colours: Travels In Mediterranean Lands
Poetic Forms

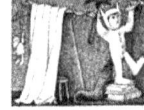

POETRY

Ursula Le Guin: Walking In Cornwall
Peter Redgrove: Here Comes The Flood
Peter Redgrove: Sex-Magic-Poetry-Cornwall
Dante: Selections From the Vita Nuova
Petrarch, Dante and the Troubadours
William Shakespeare: Sonnets
William Shakespeare: Complete Poems
Blinded By Her Light: The Love-Poetry of Robert Graves
Emily Dickinson: Selected Poems
Emily Brontë: Poems
Thomas Hardy: Selected Poems
Percy Bysshe Shelley: Poems
John Keats: Selected Poems
Joh n Keats: Poems of 1820
D.H. Lawrence: Selected Poems
Edmund Spenser: Poems
Edmund Spenser: Amoretti
John Donne: Poems
Henry Vaughan: Poems
Sir Thomas Wyatt: Poems
Robert Herrick: Selected Poems
Rilke: Space, Essence and Angels in the Poetry of Rainer Maria Rilke
Rainer Maria Rilke: Selected Poems
Friedrich Hölderlin: Selected Poems
Arseny Tarkovsky: Selected Poems
Arthur Rimbaud: Selected Poems
Arthur Rimbaud: A Season in Hell
Arthur Rimbaud and the Magic of Poetry
Novalis: Hymns To the Night
German Romantic Poetry
Paul Verlaine: Selected Poems
Elizaethan Sonnet Cycles
D.J. Enright: By-Blows
Jeremy Reed: Brigitte's Blue Heart
Jeremy Reed: Claudia Schiffer's Red Shoes
Gorgeous Little Orpheus
Radiance: New Poems
Crescent Moon Book of Nature Poetry
Crescent Moon Book of Love Poetry
Crescent Moon Book of Mystical Poetry
Crescent Moon Book of Elizabethan Love Poetry
Crescent Moon Book of Metaphysical Poetry
Crescent Moon Book of Romantic Poetry
Pagan America: New American Poetry

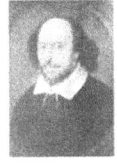
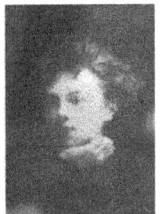
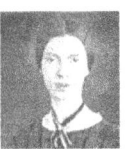
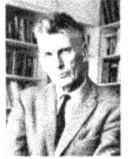
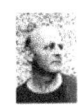
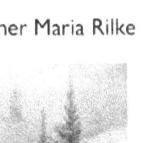
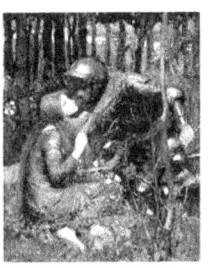
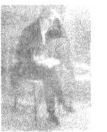
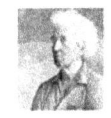
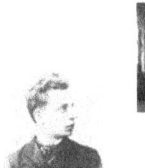
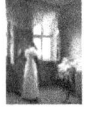

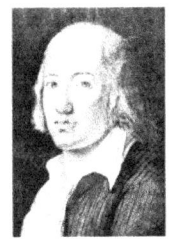
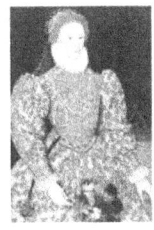

MEDIA, CINEMA, FEMINISM and CULTURAL STUDIES

J.R.R. Tolkien: The Books, The Films, The Whole Cultural Phenomenon
J.R.R. Tolkien: Pocket Guide
The *Lord of the Rings* Movies: Pocket Guide
The Cinema of Hayao Miyazaki
Hayao Miyazaki: *Princess Mononoke*: Pocket Movie Guide
Hayao Miyazaki: *Spirited Away*: Pocket Movie Guide
Tim Burton : Hallowe'en For Hollywood
Ken Russell
Ken Russell: *Tommy*: Pocket Movie Guide
The Ghost Dance: The Origins of Religion
The Peyote Cult

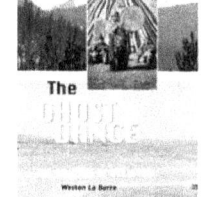
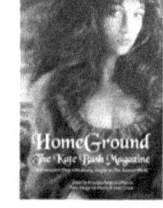

The

Cixous, Irigaray, Kristeva: The *Jouissance* of French Feminism
Julia Kristeva: Art, Love, Melancholy, Philosophy, Semiotics and Psychoanalysis
Luce Irigaray: Lips, Kissing, and the Politics of Sexual Difference
Hélene Cixous I Love You: The *Jouissance* of Writing
Andrea Dworkin
'Cosmo Woman': The World of Women's Magazines
Women in Pop Music
HomeGround: The Kate Bush Anthology
Discovering the Goddess (Geoffrey Ashe)
The Poetry of Cinema
The Sacred Cinema of Andrei Tarkovsky
Andrei Tarkovsky: Pocket Guide
Andrei Tarkovsky: *Mirror*: Pocket Movie Guide
Andrei Tarkovsky: *The Sacrifice*: Pocket Movie Guide
Walerian Borowczyk: Cinema of Erotic Dreams
Jean-Luc Godard: The Passion of Cinema
Jean-Luc Godard: *Hail Mary*: Pocket Movie Guide
Jean-Luc Godard: *Contempt*: Pocket Movie Guide
Jean-Luc Godard: *Pierrot le Fou*: Pocket Movie Guide
John Hughes and Eighties Cinema
Ferris Bueller's Day Off: Pocket Movie Guide
Jean-Luc Godard: Pocket Guide
The Cinema of Richard Linklater
Liv Tyler: Star In Ascendance
Blade Runner and the Films of Philip K. Dick
Paul Bowles and Bernardo Bertolucci
Media Hell: Radio, TV and the Press
An Open Letter to the BBC
Detonation Britain: Nuclear War in the UK
Feminism and Shakespeare
Wild Zones: Pornography, Art and Feminism
Sex in Art: Pornography and Pleasure in Painting and Sculpture
Sexing Hardy: Thomas Hardy and Feminism

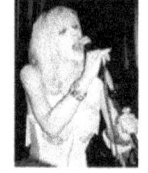
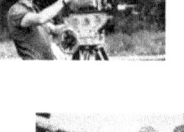
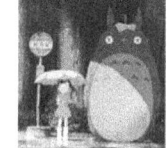
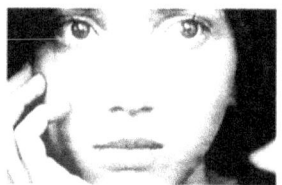

The Light Eternal is a model monograph, an exemplary job. The subject matter of the book is beautifully
organised and dead on beam. (Lawrence Durrell)
It is amazing for me to see my work treated with such passion and respect. (Andrea Dworkin)

CRESCENT MOON PUBLISHING
P.O. Box 1312, Maidstone, Kent, ME14 5XU, Great Britain. www.crmoon.com

cresmopub@yahoo.co.uk   www.crescentmoon.org.uk

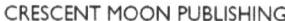